Wang Dan | 王丹

Who will cause the building to topple?

The fifty questions on China

The fifty

How should we evaluate China's
reform and opening?

questions

The fifty questions on China

Why have we established the "Dialogue
China" think-tank?

on *China*

The fifty questions on China

What is the most certain thing about China today?

The fifty questions on China

What is the social nature of China?

How to view the reality of China

About the future of China

About China's pro-democracy movement

About Taiwan, Hong Kong, Xinjiang,and Tibet

Conclusions

Preface

What are the basic issues most relevant to China today ? In September 2015, I published a book entitled 70 Questions about China, which was later reprinted with the addition of ten more questions as 80 Questions about China. Now, four years later, I am taking the two previous versions of the book as a foundation, removing some issues that are no longer relevant and adding some new issues and explanations that have cropped in recent years, I have now produced this book 50 Questions about China.

The number of questions actually is a reflection of the number of issues facing China today.

The reasons behind my writing this book are twofold. First, I feel that certain scholars in the West and in Taiwan are misleading many people with their misinterpretations of China. Second, I hope to reach all of those who care deeply about China's future development. Through this book, I hope to clarify our understanding of China.

1.

Let us first start with the China scholars.

In recent years, whether we examine economists from some Western countries, including some Nobel laureates in economics, or the so-called China experts in Taiwan, we find they have consistently presented an idyllic picture of prosperity on the mainland. This image is based on China's long-term rapid economic growth, its role as a global economic leader, the idea that it has become the manufacturing factory of the world, and the near-mythical portrayal of the power of Chinese consumption, along with images of the towering skyscrapers in Chinese cities.

Many scholars truly excel in this art of merely praising the positive.

Of course, we cannot say that everything these scholars are saying is wrong. In fact, most of their arguments can be corroborated with real-world evidence and with various data that support their views. However, the problem is that this tells only one-half of China's development story and it completely ignores the other half. There is much talk about prosperity but little mention of issues such as the erosion of labor rights. These commentators applaud the speed of construction in China but they are unwilling to mention the number of casualties due to shoddy projects. They acknowledge the economic achievements of the Chinese Communist Party (CCP) but they remain blind to its numerous political shortcomings. Although such descriptions are accurate, the methodology of these observers is flawed because only one side is presented.

Moreover, whether intentionally or unintentionally, these analysts avoid one very critical question: to what extent is what we are seeing in China genuine? This question is crucial, perhaps too crucial, which may be why it is rarely considered.

The purpose of the book is to reveal some things about China that are often overlooked due to "self-censorship." Of course, I am not claiming that what is presented here constitutes the entire truth about China, but I hope that this discussion of 50 issues related to China will serve as a necessary supplement to our thinking about China. At the very least, both positive and negative opinions should be heard, and just because our stance is one of opposition, our voices should not be ignored.

2:

Next, let us consider the students:

Young students today are becoming increasingly interested in China-related issues. After all, China is becoming closer to all of us, and it is impossible today not to care about what happens there . However, our discussions in university classrooms and in the media have traditionally been too narrow-minded when it comes to issues related to China. Our discussions about China have either focused on the relationship between Xi Jinping and the Crown Prince Party and/or his relationship with the factionalists, or about whether the "new normal" of economic growth will bring about a new Chinese "miracle" or will result in a "hard landing," and so on.

As a result: Current discussions about China mainly focus

on only two perspectives: politics and economics. I believe this is the source of our biggest misunderstanding about China. Why do I say this? Although China may be a "normal" country, Chinese society is definitely not a "normal" society. In Chinese society, there are political as well as economic distortions. If we only look at China from a political or economic perspective and ignore issues such as the collective mentality, the moral standards, the psychological issues related to the single-child generation, the historical memory of state violence, the overall prevalence of lies and deceptions, and so forth, we will never truly understand China. We would only be touching the surface and the true nature of the regime would remain obscured. No country can be truly understood by solely looking at its political and economic features, and in this respect China is certainly no different.

My goal here is to present China not only based on its political and economic qualities but also to examine issues such as culture, ethics, national characteristics, family relationships, historical memory, major events, among others, This picture of China, combined with its current political and economic features, will present a more complete representation of the country. Only with a complete picture of China can we possibly come to understand the real China today.

I must admit that deeply understanding China is a particularly challenging task because China's development has been unique and complex. I actually agree with formulation of the concept of "Chinese characteristics" proposed by the CCP. Indeed, China has its own peculiarities, making it difficult to draw simple inferences based solely on its historical experiences. I cannot claim that the 50 questions presented here necessarily encompass the entire picture about China, but I hope that through the discussion in this book, I have gone beyond the existing discourse and presented a fuller and more accurate description of China.

I know some may argue that I am only critical of the CCP, and thus I am too "radical" or simply "irrational." But, in fact, I do not accept academic statements that demand only "rationality, objectivity, and neutrality" because such viewpoints that are lacking in emotion obscure the true nature of any society, Chinese society included.

3.

I want to express here my gratitude to those many online friends who have silently supported me. Their encouragement on Facebook has been a tremendous driving force for me to continue moving forward. In particular, the earnest words from many young students in China have deeply moved and inspired me, letting me know that there is still hope for China.

I also want to thank the many teachers and mentors in Taiwan who have offered their help, especially Mr. Chen Hongzheng, who has consistently encouraged and supported me in my research and writing on China. I must give special thanks to the "Summer Star Historical Research Fund" based in the

United States for sponsoring this writing project. Without this assistance, I would not have had the leisure time to engage in the extensive reading and contemplation that became the basis for this book.

I want to thank my late mother, Ms. Wang Lingyun. During her short visit to Taiwan, although she was suffering from pneumonia, she carefully proofread the Chinese version of this book. There is no support that warms and encourages me more than the practical help I received from my mother throughout my life.

Finally, I also want to express my gratitude to all those who continuously smear, spread rumors about, and slander me, including the so-called "50 cent army" (the internet trolls). Regardless of their motives, such despicable behavior only serves one purpose for me – it motivates me to strive for greater achievements and to make more efforts to respond to their negative attacks with positive energy.

Wang Dan

About China

Question 1: Why should we distinguish between the "Chinese Communist Party" and "China"?

I once expressed regret on Facebook that there are many fewer translations and publications of Western academic works in Taiwan than there are in mainland China. But the market for translated works in Taiwan is primarily dominated by Western best-selling novels, and there is little interest in books by publishers of academic books. In this regard, books written in simplified Chinese characters have a significant advantage in terms of the selection and scope of topics. Of course, this is mainly due to the limited market for academic works in Taiwan. With fewer people reading scholarly works, publishers lack any motivation to publish them. Therefore, to gain a better understanding of Western academic developments, choosing to publish in simplified Chinese has become 1 necessary option.

Surprisingly, this discussion sparked heated debate among netizens, with many comments suggesting that translations in China are distorted and their viewpoints are concealed due to CCP control over freedom of speech.

Through this discussion on the differences in academic books between those in Taiwan and those in China, I feel that many Taiwanese friends still do not fully understand China. It is true that the Chinese authorities impose many restrictions and controls on publishing, but there are still many individuals in Chinese publishing and academic circles who have managed to bridge the gaps and translate and publish many good books for mainland audiences. For instance, in the past Guangxi Normal University Press published numerous excellent books. China is so vast, and its population is so large, that the authorities cannot completely control everything. Therefore, we should not scorn everything published in China, including private academic publications, merely because the CCP is problematic.

The fundamental problem here is that the concept of CCP governance is mixed up with the concept of China and Chinese society. Failing to distinguish between China and the CCP is a significant problem in public perceptions of China in Taiwan.

Why is it that we should not equate the Chinese people with the CCP? The reason is simple: the CCP is not elected by the Chinese people, so we cannot hold the Chinese people responsible for the actions by the CCP. Some may then ask, "Why do the Chinese people not challenge the CCP? If you, the Chinese people, tolerate the CCP government, then aren't you, the Chinese people, also responsible for it?"

To answer this question, one should consider the following. First, have the Chinese people never challenged rule by the CCP? If there had been no resistance, then what were the Chinese students doing in 1989? What were the 303 prominent intellectuals doing when they signed the "Charter 08" in 2008? What was behind the motivation of Gao Yu, who was imprisoned for a third time at the age of 71 for reporting the truth? If there had been no resistance, then what was behind Liu Xiaobo's actions? His resistance is so admired throughout the world that he was awarded the Nobel Peace Prize in 2010, thus how can one claim that the Chinese people have not resisted? It is only because the Chinese government has so actively suppressed such resistance and blocked the free flow of information that many people seem to be unaware of the ongoing resistance in China. Not knowing something does not mean that it does not exist.

Second, can't we actually ask the same question about Taiwan several decades ago? Can we really say that people in Taiwan were responsible for the White Terror because they did not resist? Certainly not. As someone who studies the history of Taiwan, I am well aware of the courageous resistance by the likes of Peng Ming-min and Lin Yi-hsiung and the prices they paid to stick to their convictions.

Taiwan underwent the same stages of democratization that China is undergoing today. Think about it, during the Formosa Incident, many people in Taiwan thought of themselves as outlaws or bandits. Shouldn't the people in Taiwan who have already gone down the road of democratization encourage and support the mainlanders and not look down upon them or assert that they cannot be successful. Shouldn't the people in Taiwan have open-minded attitudes?

Today, Taiwan has elections, and Ma Ying-jeou was elected through a majority vote (even if it was not an overwhelming majority, it was still a majority). Nevertheless, if I were to claim that Ma Ying-jeou's government represents all people in Taiwan, I am sure many netizens would vehemently oppose such a statement.

Think about it, even a government elected by a majority vote, many people do not believe it represents all of the people in Taiwan. In China where there are no elections at all, is it fair to equate the entire population with the CCP? If we do this, how can we truly understand the real China?

Question 2: What is the most certain thing about China today?

Here, I want to address a fundamental issue that is important to any understanding of China and I also want to present my own views. I believe that there are a vast number of complex issues to understand and in order to make sense of them, it is crucial to have a clear methodological approach. Having clear principles enables us calmly and rationally to analyze the myriad of issues surrounding China.

The first principle among these fundamental issues is the issue of uncertainty. In my view, the most definite judgment one can make about China today is its uncertainty.

I often encounter questions like, "How many more years will there be before you think China will change?" To be frank, my answer is simply "I don't know." In other words, if anyone thinks they are able to provide a specific answer to this question, it would be very strange indeed!

The unpredictability of China stems primarily from its massive scale and elaborate complexity, making it difficult for any external observers to unify all the problems and to make one final judgment. Additionally, in any political entity of such an immense size, there are numerous unpredictable factors and unexpected events that may occur at any time, making it a challenging task to determine the final development path. A significant amount of the information and data we do have, especially related to the inner workings of the CCP, remains under the strict control of the Chinese authorities. This opacity leads to only a foggy understanding among outsiders. As a result, we cannot accurately predict what changes might occur in China in the future.

Taking the history of the CCP as an example: when the high-level leadership, including Jiang Qing, was collectively eliminated in October 1976, even the day before only a handful of party officials at the provincial and ministerial levels knew about the impending purge that was about to take place the following day. This says nothing about the ordinary citizens, both inside and outside of China, who had even less access to high-level information. China experienced an overnight transformation, and aside from the few individuals involved in the high-level decision-making regarding the forthcoming coup, no one could have predicted the exact timing of the event, to say nothing of whether it would even take place. As another example, just one week prior to Bo Xilai's detention and investigation, he was confidently speaking to domestic and foreign journalists at the "Two Sessions." At the time, who could have confidently predicted that he was about to be imprisoned?

The existence of these uncertainties has an underlying logic, as I mentioned earlier: the immense scale of the Chinese political system and the secrecy of all operations in the system. Indeed, it is only these two factors, the immense scale and the secrecy of operations, that are certainties. Therefore, all I can say is the most certain thing about China is its uncertainty.

Recognizing the uncertainty surrounding Chinese politics and development has important implications, or rather presents a certain necessity. It helps us to objectively examine the various possibilities facing Chinese development. However, the existence of uncertainty is not necessarily a bad thing, as it implies the presence of various possibilities, including possibilities that may turn out to be surprising. If we agree with this principle, then we can make the following two judgments:

First, there is no reason to believe that China's political development in the short term at least will follow a normal linear trajectory, meaning that economic development will inevitably lead to democracy. From the long-term perspective of human history, I firmly believe that China in the future will eventually move in the direction of a constitutional democratic political arrangement. However, in the short term, starting from the principle of uncertainty, we cannot rule out the possibility that China will continue in its current state or even regress politically.

Second, at the same time, starting from uncertainty we have no reason to believe that the possibility of a trend in the direction of Chinese democratization in China in the short term does not exist. Perhaps we lack specific and highly reliable evidence to prove that a democratic transformation may occur in the short term, but in the face of a regime and a country where surface appearances often diverge significantly from the reality, we clearly cannot reach absolute negative conclusions simply because we cannot present precise counter-evidence.

Perhaps these two conclusions seem contradictory, but in actuality they reflect the reality of China today: a country and society entangled in contradictions, currently standing at the crossroads of various possibilities. China's fate will depend on the interactions among various political and social variables during this critical transitional period.

Question 3: Will those who govern based on their own self-interest inevitably perish?

The model of governance of the Chinese Communist Party (CCP) has undergone several transformations: with the founding of the People's Republic in 1949, Mao Zedong set China on a political path whereby the CCP was an ideological animal relying on the cult of the individual and working the entire country into a political frenzy. Enthusiasm was abundant but ungrounded. In the end, the illusion vanished and the people came to realize that it was due to Mao's policies that China had become destitute. The CCP model then underwent a fundamental shift under Deng Xiaoping in 1978, substituting the former political path for "economic development at the center." This guiding principle was carried out from Deng to Jiang Zemin and from Jiang to Hu Jintao. Today, however, Xi Jinping puts more weight on politics. But, at least for now, he has not completely undone the model of governance set in place by Deng.

What does it mean to put "economic development at the center"? In truth, it refers to a world established through the barrel of a gun, maintained through the dividing up of interests. In the process of economic development, officials at all levels of government are complicit, and corruption and bribery are the driving forces behind reform, leading to the formation of massive interest groups across various sectors. Even ordinary people manage to reap some benefits.. After 1989 Deng introduced what I call "rule by profit." Its basic logic is simple and therefore effective: as long as you support the CCP's autocratic rule, you will benefit. Idealists are a minority in every society, whether they are officials at various levels or the majority of ordinary people. Most people are more concerned about tangible benefits; making money is more important than preserving dignity. This is human nature, and it is not the fault of the Chinese people.

Official corruption will give rise to two lingering issues. First, rest   assured that the people have also benefited from economic   development – but they are also human, with human flaws such as the   tendency to never be content with one's lot and always to compare one's   situation to that of others. Even though your life might have improved, if
you see that other people (especially officials) are living much better than you are, you will still be dissatisfied and ultimately you will come to hate corruption. The CCP has brought many gains to the people, but the people still hate party officials. It may seem that they are ungrateful, but this is merely human nature. Second, the CCP relies on utilizing benefits to attract and stabilize the official ranks, but it thereby inadvertently nurtures various interest groups. If you think this is an absolute positive for the CCP, think again. No position is more troublesome, or more perilous, than that of a gang leader who is sharing the spoils. The CCP has to be careful how it slices the pie, especially among these various interest groups. As soon as one feels he has not gotten his fair share, a political fight is inevitable. The takedown of Zhou Yongkang, Ling Jihua, and others by thein the Crown Prince Party and Bo Xilai's "strike black" campaign in Chongqing, were essentially both about the distribution of benefits. These political disputes all resulted from the uneven

distribution of interests.

Economic growth keeps conflict at bay. There is not much grumbling when there are plenty of profits to spread around. But if the economy takes a dive, the CCP will have less to share and much more to worry about. China is facing the latter scenario right now. But the CCP created this trouble in the first place. If you rule by profit, you die by profit. That is dialectical materialism.

Question 4: What will the political situation be in China during the next five years?

The 20th Chinese Communist Party (CCP) National Congress (in October of 2022) opened with Xi Jinping delivering a political report on behalf of the 19th CCP Politburo. Generally, this report has been full of hackneyed words and jargon, and it usually is as dry as dust, a tasteless and dull Communist Party report. However, if we carefully examine the full text, we will find some possible clues about Xi Jinping's political thinking about the future. In my opinion, there are three key words in this report that deserve the attention

The first key word is the word "struggle." Based on statistical reporting on the internet, this word is mentioned a number of times. The four takeaways from the speech include: We will not back down from zero-Covid; Economic development will involve an uphill battle; There will be increased pressure on Taiwan; and China's global ambitions will continue. When referring to the central task for the next five to ten years, Xi said that the entire CCP and the entire country should "prepare for a major test on stormy seas." He also said that in order to prepare, we must "rely on a tenacious struggle to open up new horizons in our business development." The problem is: What is this shocking wave that will require such an emphasis on "struggle"? Will it be a struggle within the CCP or a war between China and the United States? Xi Jinping does not explicitly say, but whatever it is, the repeated emphasis on "struggle" runs counter to his claim of a "peaceful rise" for China. The emphasis on struggle also reveals the political character of this second generation of Red Guards, who grew up drinking the wolf's milk of the Cultural Revolution and is full of the spirit of the Red Guards. This is also a reflection of Xi's feeling of fear.

Most of Xi Jinping's political report is full of old concepts, but there is one relatively new concept that is worth noting – "Chinese modernization" – which I regard as the second keyword. That is to say, during his term of office, Xi Jinping will try to establish a Chinese model for the modernization of human society that is different from the Western model. The main content of this model is "common prosperity." This will probably be the main focus of the Communist Party's propaganda and the so-called "Xi Jinping Thought" in the future. I think it reflects a further expansion of Xi Jinping's ambition to "create a new form of human civilization," as he puts it in his report. Xi Jinping is thus not only trying to direct all aspects of China's social development but in the future also to direct all of human development. This is of course a replication of Chairman Mao's ambition to become the "leader of the workers of the world." It is clear that Xi Jinping's mind has developed an arrogance born of ignorance. If such arrogance continues, it will be a threat to both China and the world.

The third keyword repeatedly emphasized in Xi's report is "the people." In addition to the very familiar phrase "state power is the power of the people." Xi Jinping adds: "To defend state power is to defend the hearts of the people." This is simply an empty phrase. I believe Xi Jinping himself does not know what he is talking about. But the word "defend" here, I think, actually is meant not to convey the idea of "protecting" but rather to convey the idea of control and restraint. The term the "people" is also used repeatedly. This was an important theme that Xi Jinping dwelled upon when he first came to power in 2012, and now, over ten years later, I am afraid it still is a central theme in the so-called "Xi Jinping Thought." Old dogs really cannot learn new tricks. However, it might be a foreshadowing of the fact that in the future rule by Xi might focus on populism, that is, social policies aimed at pleasing the grassroots by improving the people's livelihood. Common prosperity represents an embodiment of such policies, which essentially rob the rich to help the poor by attacking the landlords and dividing up their property. I believe that after listening to this report, many rich people in China have accelerated their efforts to transfer their capital abroad.

In general, the political regression of the past decade under Xi Jinping's rule is reflected in the increase in the amount of state control over society. Whereas the economic regression has been highlighted by "the advance of the state at the expense of the people" [國進民退] and a resurgence of attacks against landlords and the dividing up of their property, the key elements of Xi Jinping's future rule are likely to feature a new political struggle in confrontation with mainstream civilization.

But will China really revert back to the dark ages? Not necessarily.

On the eve of the CCP's 20th National Congress, at Sitong (Stone) Bridge in Beijing's Haidian District, someone hung two banners: one reading "We don't want nucleic acid testing (Covid tests), we want food to eat; We don't want lockdowns, we want freedom; We don't want lies, we want dignity; We don't want another Cultural Revolution, we want reform; We don't want [dictatorial] leaders, we want elections; We don't want to be slaves, we want to be citizens; and the other banner reading: "Go on strike at school and at work, remove dictator and national traitor Xi Jinping!"

It is still uncertain who did this. Some say it is Twitter user Peng Zaizhou, but this has not yet been confirmed.

To be able to pull off such a feat at such a sensitive moment, this lone protester, who beforehand must have given this act much thought, was willing to pay a huge price because he must have known that the authorities would not let him get away with it. In such dark times, when almost everyone is forced to remain silent, the fact that this brave man was willing to come forward was so moving that it shook heaven and earth. Thus, it is not unreasonable to call him the tank man of the twenty-first century, similar to the lone man who stood in front of the tanks in 1989. Regardless of his personal fate, this feat will be written in the history books, and it will tell the future generations that even in the darkest of times, there were still people in China who were willing to stand up.

Although this act of courage was very inspiring, I do not

think it will not bring about any immediate change to China. People will not take to the streets tomorrow in large numbers. But regardless, this event is still significant.

First, for so many years, outsiders have regarded the Chinese people as a cynical, cowardly group of people and as slaves who dare not resist. But this simply is not true. Under Xi's comprehensive and brutal rule with Chinese characteristics, the difficulties of resistance are beyond the comprehension of the outside world. Because we resisted in Beijing in 1989, we have had to pay the price of not being able to return home. This is an indication of how difficult it is to resist in today's China. Those outside critics should have some empathy. If you were living in China, would you dare to resist? If you yourself would not dare to resist, then how are you qualified to criticize the Chinese people? However, even under such circumstances, there are still Chinese people, like Liu Xiaobo, Li Wangyang, and the brave unknown man on Sitong Bridge, who, in the face of great danger and pressure, stood up and resisted without regard for their personal lives, revealing that the Chinese people want democracy. This is important because there is somewhat of a perception in the international community that the Chinese do not want democracy and do not deserve support. The action by the brave man on Sitong Bridge shows that such a perception is completely incorrect.

Second, the brave man who stood up on Sitong bridge was actually registering his opposition to Xi Jinping's re-election to a third term in office. Xi's third term is a development that is completely unacceptable to many Chinese people. So the banner unfurled by this brave man was an expression of the feelings of many Chinese people. It reflected the anxiety and despair in the hearts of the people. Finally, Xi Jinping was called a "national traitor." Some people say that this protest action will not change anything. Whether or not this is the case, just by shouting out the thoughts of the people, the action will be recorded in the history books. This represents the second important significance of this great feat.

Third, this protester may be a lone hero who struggles against many, and it may be that we will not see more people taking to the streets anytime soon. But things always start with "1" and expand to 10,000. At the beginning, there were only 300 signatories to the hunger strike proclamation in Tiananmen Square in 1989, but later the number expanded to 3,000. and even 10 million people took to the streets. For an opposition movement, a role model is particularly important. As long as someone is bravely willing to take a first step, it is not difficult to expect that more people will follow. This kind of courage, at the great cost of personal sacrifice, is the key to the success of any social movement. This is the third significance of his brave act.

Fourth, Xi Jinping may have been re-elected to a third term, but this brave man's actions are a harbinger of things to come. It is a sign that – with Xi Jinping's dictatorship and resistance and rebellion against him coming from all sides – the next five years will see the development of a new trend in Chinese politics. Anxiety and despair are, to a certain extent, healthy signs, and it is only when people no longer have any hope that rebellion becomes possible. The result of despair may be the emergence of more warriors like Peng Zaihou.

For a long time I have said that Xi Jinping's third term is unlikely to go smoothly, and he will probably not reach a fourth term. I think the occurrence of this event is evidence.

Question 5: What Are Three Misunderstandings about China?

When it comes to China, there are many misunderstandings due to its vast size and complex history, making it difficult for outsiders to grasp its true nature. In order to better understand China, we need to more deeply analyze the surface phenomena and grasp the true pulse of the country. Here, I will provide three examples for discussion:

Example 1: Many people claim that Chinese, especially those of the younger generation, are indifferent to politics and social affairs. They are seen as only caring about themselves, thus leading some to conclude there is no hope for democracy in China. Is that really the case? Definitely not!

Superficially, it may appear to be the case, and upon closer analysis, it is not illogical. Across cultures and generations, the youth typically have been among the most enthusiastic and most idealistic. Curiosity about the outside world is inherent in human nature and naturally such a curiosity does not bypass politics. If there is any indifference among the youth, it is the result of external factors and not due to genuine apathy.

Moreover, the political enthusiasm of Chinese youth has been suppressed by the objective environment. Open discussions of politics can lead to interrogation by the authorities, and any expression of deeper political concerns often comes at the cost of one's personal freedom. This is especially the case in China after the brutal crackdown on the Tiananmen Square protesters. Similar phenomena occurred in Taiwan during the period of "White Terror," and such behavior is not unique to China. It is a common worldwide response to any oppressive regime.

Furthermore, history has shown that whenever external repression or political constraints ease in China, enthusiasm for politics resurfaces. The Cultural Revolution, for instance, saw a surge in political passions when the youth were allowed to participate freely. Today's political apathy is a consequence of the renewed restrictions and external factors, and it not due to a genuine lack of political interest. The fascination with political gossip today is actually an expression of a distorted political enthusiasm.

In conclusion, the notion that the "Chinese people are indifferent to politics" is a typical misunderstanding that fails to grasp the real situation in China. The current emergence of political apathy is a result of various complex factors and not a genuine reflection of the true sentiments of the Chinese people

Example 2: Many people believe that most Chinese support the current regime. However, this is a misconception that lacks reliable evidence. Elections are the basic benchmark to gauge government support, but China lacks genuine elections. Therefore, there is no way to know whether the people really support the government because dissident voices are suppressed and there are numerous political taboos. In addition, because of the limits on free speech, it is also difficult to conduct any reliable surveys.

Even if it seems that the regime has widespread support, it is crucial to analyze how such support is obtained. Some may seem to genuinely support the CCP, but they may be feigning support due to coercion or personal gain. In an authoritarian state, coerced support is actually unreliable as it lacks true loyalty. Furthermore, some may support the regime for pragmatic reasons and because they see no viable alternative or hope for change. This is known as "cynical obedience," and it is not genuine support.

Therefore, the notion that the "Chinese people overwhelmingly support the CCP" is an unfounded claim. It is important to recognize that what appears as support is often coerced or opportunistic, and it does not reflect genuine backing.

Example 3: People believe that Chinese have forgotten about the Tiananmen Square massacre (June 4th incident). However, this is a misconception as well. Although it is true that China's younger generation might not know all the details about the event, a sizable portion of the population, especially those over the age of 40, still remembers. The event was a national tragedy that involved a substantial proportion of the population, making it impossible for the majority to forget.

Though people might not openly discuss June 4th due to fears of reprisal, it does not mean that they have forgotten. In fact, suppression of information has led to further curiosity, especially among the younger generation, who are eager to explore any taboo subject. As long as the Chinese government continues to suppress information about June 4th , the people's curiosity will persist, making it impossible for them to forget.

In conclusion, the belief that "Chinese people have forgotten about June 4th is a superficial observation that fails to understand the psychological impact of suppressed history. The memory remains, and as long as the event remains taboo, people's curiosity will continue to keep the memory alive.

Question 6: What is the social nature of China?

When I taught at National Tsing Hua University in Taiwan, at the beginning of each semester I would hold a "China Salon." During these gatherings, I would ask the students from China and Taiwan a fundamental question: What is the social nature of China? I believe that this is a crucial judgment we must make when trying to understand China.

The students' responses varied widely: some said it is oligarchic capitalism, some called it an authoritarian society, some referred to it as socialism with Chinese characteristics, and others described it as a hybrid of capitalism and socialism. In my view, all these answers have some truth to them but none of them are entirely accurate. Regarding China's social nature, that is, what kind of country China is today, it is difficult to provide a completely positive characterization because various elements of different social natures coexist in modern China, and no single characterization can encompass all of them. Although we cannot give a comprehensive positive characterization, I believe it is important to understand the nature of Chinese society through a process of negative elimination. The negative elimination results are as follows:

First, it is incorrect to claim that China today is a socialist country. Throughout history, from Saint-Simon to Fourier, from Marx to Lenin, the core essence of socialism has been described as equality of wealth. However, in today's China, the wealth gap is enormous, which goes against the principle of an equal distribution of wealth under socialism. During the Stalin and Mao era, the principles of socialism emphasized the dictatorship of the proletariat, meaning that the working class should hold absolute power within the political system. However, in today's China, the so-called "proletariat," which is the working class, is not the leading social force; rather, the working class is now being exploited by the privileged elite. Hence, it is inappropriate to call China a socialist country.

Second, it is also incorrect to label China as a capitalist country. Whether it is oligarchic capitalism or capitalism with socialist characteristics, the core essence of either is still capitalism. Capitalism is not merely about economic relations and productive forces; it also encompasses human relationships, the relationship between state and society and the interplay between planning and the market. In today's China, all of these characteristics are absent. The number of state-owned enterprises in the national economy far exceeds the number of private enterprises. Based on this fact alone, claiming that China has already entered the ranks of the capitalist countries is simply a joke. This is also the fundamental reason why Europe, the United States, and Japan refuse to recognize China as a market economy. Additionally, capitalism as a social system has more profound connotations, including constraints of religious ethics on capital in social development and checks and balances between political arrangements and economic systems, none of which are at all evident in today's China. Therefore, it is completely baseless to state that China has acquired a capitalist nature.

If the above analysis holds true, then we would know that China is neither strictly a socialist country nor is it strictly a capitalist country. In reality, it is somewhat of an enigma with elements of various natures, but it cannot be defined by any single system. Perhaps this is a characteristic of China during its transitional period.

The significance of pointing this out is that many people who have high expectations about China's transformation, especially scholars in the West countries, believe that China has already entered the stage of capitalist development, even if it is oligarchic capitalism. This erroneous judgment leads to false expectations: assuming that it is a capitalist country, the country should naturally follow the logic of capital and formulate national development plans based on reason and self-interest. The result of capitalist development should be the rise of a middle class and an urgent demand for democracy. This logic forms the theoretical basis of the hope, among many Western scholars who study China, that China's ruling group will eventually move in the direction of democratization. Unfortunately, the facts have already proven them to be wrong. China has become powerful, but it has not moved toward democracy. What I want to say here is that one fundamental reason for this misjudgment by Western scholars about China's development is that they are overly wishful when characterizing China's social nature.

About the Chinese Communist Party

Question 7: How can we understand the Chinese Communist Party?

On July 1, 2021, the Chinese Communist Party (CCP) celebrated its 100th anniversary, and it took that opportunity for self-praise and to emphasize its "great, glorious, and correct" characteristics. Such self-praise, however, has lost any credibility, and even the members of the CCP propaganda teams probably do not believe the words they write. Nevertheless, the establishment of the CCP and its one-hundred-year history have had, and continue to have, a significant impact on China's development. Although we may not agree with the saying that "without the Communist Party, there would be no new China," it is undeniable that China would be quite different today if it were not for the CCP.

One must acknowledge that ever since its inception the CCP has consistently had one distinct characteristic – that is, its "violent nature." The CCP worships and relies on violence to establish, expand, and maintain its political power. Because the party relies on violence, there are no conditions in China that will allow it to evolve into a modern political party that seeks peaceful solutions to societal conflicts. Even in 1989, forty years after taking power, when people were demanding reform, the

CCP responded with violence. Violence has become this party's habitual approach to deal with any problem.

Moreover, violence has not only been a common characteristic of CCP behavior but it has also deeply influenced CCP thinking, resulting in a political line that is inherently violent. This influence began in its early days and it has continually been strengthened over the past one hundred years, resulting in a path dependence that the CCP cannot escape. Recognition of this fact is crucial because only by understanding the CCP's violent nature can we abandon any false illusions about the regime and face the challenging and costly task of ending China's one-party rule.

Regarding the legitimacy of the CCP, although it has been in power for 72 years, the regime lacks any procedural legitimacy. The CCP came to power through armed revolution and it did not undergo one of the most basic standards for legitimacy, that is, elections. Although many countries recognize the People's Republic of China, regime legitimacy is not solely based on international recognition; it also requires recognition by its own people. But the CCP has never proven its legitimacy through a legal process or through elections, and the Chinese people have never had an opportunity to freely express their choices through voting.

Furthermore, the nature of the CCP is vastly different from that of a modern political party. Modern parties are tied intrinsically to elections, whereby the members of the party identify with their party during the time of elections. However, the CCP does not follow this model. Its leadership is not elected; rather it is recommended and appointed through a top-down process. The top leader holds dictatorial power not unlike that of China's feudal emperors, and loyalty to the party as well as to its leader is emphasized above all else. The CCP's governing style is more akin to that of a feudal organization than it is to a modern political party.

Another characteristic of the CCP is its "inherent inadequacy and subsequent dysfunction." When the CCP was founded, its early leaders, despite their idealism, came to adopt an expedient mindset focused on achieving power and greatness for China. This led them to abandon long-term enlightenment efforts and to embrace socialism due to their admiration for the Soviet experiment. This shift prioritized collective interests over individual freedoms and imposed strict discipline on party members, emphasizing party loyalty more than anything else. As a result, historically the CCP has been "left leaning." and it has not been able to implement any democratic reforms or to make any self-corrections due to its reliance on violence and its militaristic mindset.

In conclusion, the CCP is not a modern political party. Rather, it is a large-scale gang-like organization under the guise of a political party. Its violent nature, lack of procedural legitimacy, and feudal-like governing style, as well as its inherent inadequacy and subsequent dysfunction, have influenced China's development for over a century. As we reflect on the CCP's 100 years, it is essential for every Chinese person to think about how we can bring about an end to one-party rule and how we can embrace democratic reforms to create a better future.

Question 8: Why is today's Chinese Communist Party described as "corrupt but invincible"?

How do we view the Chinese Communist Party (CCP), which governs a country with a population of 1.4 billion? How do we perceive its current and future state? I believe that "corrupt but invincible" is an apt and profound description.

The term "corrupt" naturally refers to a state of corruption. After Xi Jinping took office, the outside world started to believe that he was raising the banner of anti-corruption, seemingly bringing hope for change to the CCP. However, this was merely wishful thinking. Not only did Xi Jinping's anti-corruption campaign not target the underlying system causing the corruption but it also was very selective in its actions, making it unlikely that it would achieve its goals. The key point is that the vast rent-seeking space created by corruption remains the main resource for the CCP to co-opt and absorb the social elites. If it were to become a truly clean party, the party would most likely then become isolated. Corruption has become the lifeblood of the CCP.

Regarding the CCP's corruption, there is also another layer of meaning: This old party, over ninety years old, may still appear lush and majestic on the outside, but it is like an ancient tree with numerous wounds and decay on the inside. Today, there are still many young people who want to join the party, but it is clear that they do so for their own self-interest and career prospects. In other words, they hope to gain benefits from the party rather than actually having any genuine belief in the party. Such a party, as long as it can maintain its current state, may appear to be steadfast. But once it comes up against any challenges, it may instantly collapse. The reason is simple: it is already "decayed on the inside."

However, at the same time, we must recognize that the current CCP, despite its being corrupt and decayed, has not yet reached a point of total defeat. In fact, it is still far from being defeated. There are numerous reasons for this, which we cannot comprehensively analyze here, but we can briefly list a few.

Apart from the significant rent-seeking space created by corruption that forms a solid economic foundation for CCP rule, the CCP's immense resources enable it to calmly confront any economic crises. Those who believe that the Chinese economy will collapse due to an inability to boost domestic demand underestimate the complexity of this issue. In reality, the vast administrative expenditures of the state alone are sufficient to generate huge domestic demand. As an analogy, the old banyan tree located at National Cheng Kung University in Tainan City, Taiwan, which is also the logo of Cathay United Bank and is where the students enjoy studying in its shade, is a century-old tree that appears to be lush and green. During my time working at the university, I knew that annual maintenance of the tree required considerable funds from the school and even the bank to keep the tree healthy and alive. In other words, if there were to come a day when there is no money for maintenance, the old tree will not last for very long. Similarly, the CCP, even as an apparently healthy tree, incurs exceedingly high costs to maintain its façade of robust health.

Moreover, the societal crisis has not yet reached a point whereby can shake the regime. As mentioned earlier, the CCP will instantly collapse when faced with a crisis, but China has not yet reached that turbulent moment. Such a moment will require the growth and maturity of other conditions, such as a strong and awakened middle class, courageous acts by a minority of individuals, internal disintegration within the ruling class, and international pressures, among others. I believe that these conditions will gradually accumulate, but until they become ripe, the CCP will not fall, no matter how corrupt it may be.

Understanding the current state of the CCP as "corrupt but invincible" helps us to view China's future correctly. Some people may think that the social contradictions in China have worsened, that the time for transformation is ripe, and that a social revolution will erupt within the next three to five years. I believe this perspective sees only the "corrupt" side but fails to recognize the reasons for the current "invincibility" of the regime. Others believe that CCP rule is unshakeable, but they overlook the internal decay beneath its outward appearance of strength. In my view, the state of being "corrupt but invincible" means that the CCP regime will not immediately plunge into crisis, and we may witness the current state for an extended period of time into the future. However, due to its inherent decay, its downfall is inevitable; nevertheless, it is challenging, or even impossible, to predict the exact timing. Therefore, with respect to China's future, I am neither pessimistic nor optimistic; I can only be patient.

Question 9: Was Deng Xiaoping truly the "chief architect" of China's reform and opening?

When referring to Deng Xiaoping, he is generally regarded as the "chief architect" of China's reform and opening – the decision-maker who made the shift from Mao Zedong's class struggle to a new governing philosophy focusing on economic development. According to the biography of Deng Xiaoping written by Harvard professor Ezra F. Vogel, Deng Xiaoping led China forward into a new era. But was this really the case? To answer this, some historical clarifications are necessary.

A well-known phrase used to describe China's reform and opening is "crossing the river by feeling for the stones." It is meant to describe the main strategy that opened up the 1980s reform policy and it is also a prominent element in the so-called "Deng Xiaoping Theory" that is frequently cited in official CCP discourse. However, Deng Xiaoping never uttered this phrase, and it was never even proposed during the reform and opening period.

The person who proposed this theory was none other than Chen Yun, known as China's "economic czar." Chen Yun is regarded as a conservative leader who supported the planned economy during the reform years of the 1980s . He first mentioned this phrase in the 1950s. On April 7, 1950, during the 27th Executive Meeting of the State Council, in a discussion on the issue of rising prices, Chen Yun said, "It is not good for prices to rise or to fall too much. Last month, prices fell by 5 percent. We should control this by decreasing first and increasing later, thereby stabilizing prices. We should cross the river by feeling for the stones and proceed cautiously." On July 20, 1951, during a discussion of the United Front Work Department of the CCP Central Committee on how to handle work with the All-China Industrial and Commercial Federation, Chen Yun again referred to the phrase "crossing the river by feeling for the stones." Since then, this phrase has become very well-known within the CCP. Marshal Liu Bocheng once told General Zhang Aiping, who was tasked with setting up the military academies, "I'll give you six words to remember firmly: "Cross the river by feeling for the stones."

Thereafter, Chen Yun no longer was in charge of overseeing economic policies and he was gradually sidelined by Mao Zedong. But after Deng Xiaoping came to power, Chen Yun regained some influence in the formulation of China's economic policies. Almost thirty years later, one of Chen Yun's most significant policy proposals remained "crossing the river by feeling for the stones." On December 16, 1980, during the opening ceremony of the CCP Central Work Conference, Chen Yun again stated, "Reform certainly requires theoretical research, economic statistics, and economic predictions. But more importantly, reform should start with trial implementation and the summing up of experiences, that is, crossing the river by feeling for the stones."

Looking back at this history, it is important to trace the true origin of the phrase. The results of such an investigation will be thought-provoking. They will indicate that we need to re-evaluate the role of Deng Xiaoping and the reform and opening of China that he supposedly initiated.

First, "crossing the river by feeling for the stones" was not an original invention by Deng Xiaoping; he was merely repeating Chen Yun's viewpoint. So Deng should not get credit for the formulation of this crucial strategy that directed the 1980s reforms. Furthermore, actual implementation of this strategy can be said to be the achievement of the two general secretaries of the CCP prior to and after Deng Xiaoping, that is, Hu Yaobang and Zhao Ziyang. Therefore, the extent of Deng Xiaoping's role in promoting the reforms of the 1980s needs to be re-evaluated.

More importantly, as noted, the phrase "crossing the river by feeling for the stones" was a proposal for development from the 1950s. The Deng Xiaoping–style reforms, in fact, actually were a continuation of early CCP policies, or what is known as the "new democracy," that is, moderately protecting and developing capitalism and not rushing to transition to socialism. Evaluations of Deng Xiaoping, and the reforms that he led, such as "opening a new era" or "entering a new period," are overly complimentary and not in line with the facts. The Deng Xiaoping–style reforms did not push China forward; rather, they took China back to the 1950s.

The imprint of the development approach of the early 1950s deeply marked the collective leadership of the CCP for generations, enduring to this day and including the leadership of

Xi Jinping. To some extent, Xi Jinping is also going backward, attempting to return to the 1950s to find experiences to maintain his rule. A true re-evaluation of Deng Xiaoping involves an understanding of the imprint of the reality of the 1950s on the Deng Xiaoping–style reforms.

Question 10: What are the differences between my ideas and those of Prof. Ezra Vogel regarding Deng Xiaoping?

Regarding Deng Xiaoping, the late Prof. Vogel, an authority on East Asian studies at my alma mater Harvard University, published a Chinese translation of his book on Deng Xiaoping in Taiwan that offers many insights and made a historical evaluation of Deng Xiaoping. Prof. Vogel had long been devoted to studying issues related to China, and while his perspectives have their unique merits, there also some viewpoints that I find erroneous, reflecting more generally some misconceptions among some Western China scholars

My most significant disagreement with Prof. Vogel is his sympathetic and understanding stance with respect to Deng Xiaoping's decision to use military force to suppress the 1989 pro-democracy movement. Prof. Vogel believed that "from the perspective of China's unity and the foundation of Chinese Communist Party (CCP) rule, there were no better options at that time" and that "in retrospect, this judgment might have been right, especially for China at that time." I believe this conclusion fundamentally contradicts the facts and is a wishful judgment that is biased in favor of the CCP.

In 1989, thousands of students staged a hunger strike in Tiananmen Square, triggering a nationwide pro-democracy movement. Was there really no other way for the ruling authorities to handle the situation apart from resorting to violence? Of course not! The students' demands, including calling for an end to corruption and the resignation of certain officials, were reasonable and legitimate. The two main demands during the hunger strike were to engage in a dialogue with the government and to revise the "April 26" editorial. These were entirely achievable demands that the government could have accepted without causing China to fall apart.

If the authorities had accepted these two students' two demands, there would have been no reason for the students to continue their hunger strike and the situation could have easily been defused. Isn't that a better way to resolve the issue? Perhaps Prof. Vogel believed that the CCP would never make any concessions, so such an option was unrealistic. However, at that time, Zhao Ziyang, general secretary of the CCP, was already prepared to take a more lenient approach and partially accept the students' demands. Therefore, it was not an impossible scenario. It was only later when Deng Xiaoping and Li Peng launched a coup and forced Zhao Ziyang to step down that the possibility for such a scenario was shattered. Clearly, the situation was not as Prof. Vogel described in his claim that "there were no better options at that time." In reality, the better options were rejected, leading to the tragic outcome. And the one who rejected these options was none other than Deng Xiaoping.

Prof. Ezra Vogel's evaluation of Deng Xiaoping actually reflects the same misconceptions that are found among some other Western experts on China. They do not take a stand based on right and wrong or on universal values. Instead, they tend to empathize with the perspective of the authoritarian rulers and prioritize political realism over universal values. Prof. Vogel mentioned "putting oneself in the other's shoes" to justify his support for Deng Xiaoping's actions. This surprises me. Deng Xiaoping was the dictator of an authoritarian country who was willing to shed blood to suppress its people, and Prof. Vogel was a highly esteemed scholar in the West. Why would he choose to think from the perspective of a dictator?

When I was studying at Harvard, I had many interactions with Prof. Vogel and I often attended his lectures. During the time he was drafting his book on Deng Xiaoping, he even interviewed me so I should address him as "teacher." However, there is an old Chinese saying, "I love my teacher, but I love the truth more." Therefore, I cannot refrain from openly questioning Prof. Vogel's academic judgment: If making the decision to suppress the students with military force was deemed to be the right choice for Deng Xiaoping based on unity and continued party rule, then what reason do we have to condemn the Nazi massacre of the Jews? Hitler also justified his actions by saying they would contribute to the rise of Germany.

More importantly, I would like to ask why, when making judgments, would a Western scholar focus on the stability of an authoritarian regime rather than on the value of human lives?

Of course, I must also note that my article on this topic, which in fact publicly criticizes Prof. Vogel's work, was later translated into English and brought to his attention. Upon reading my article, he personally wrote to me, expressing his disagreement but without any tone at all of resentment. He even indicated his willingness to continue our discussion. Such scholarly conduct is commendable, and we should not invalidate someone's worth based on words alone.

Question 11: Who was Xi Jinping's father?

When readers see this question, they might think it is a pointless question. Of course, Xi Jinping is the son of Xi Zhongxun. From a bloodline perspective, that is absolutely correct. However, when discussing Xi Jinping's political legacy, it is not about his bloodline and that is worthy of discussion.

Even before Xi Jinping took office, many people were interested in the question of "Who was Xi Jinping's father?" Their interest was due to the fact that Xi Jinping's father, Xi Zhongxun, was considered a representative of the reformist faction within the Chinese Communist Party (CCP). Therefore, many people wondered whether Xi Jinping might have been influenced by his father, leading to certain expectations. The commemoration of Xi Zhongxun's centenary by the CCP further fueled these expectations. Clearly, any discussion about "Who was Xi Jinping's father?" focuses on the transmission of an ideological legacy. The general belief is that having a reformist father like Xi Zhongxun would mean that Xi Jinping would carry on the spirit of reform.

If such logic were valid, political science would be reduced to genetics.

Assuming that children will inherit the same mindset and ideas as their parents lacks a logical foundation. Moreover, in the context of the CCP, such assumptions not only do not exist but in fact they are often reversed. Former Premier Li Peng, for example, was the adopted son of CCP founding elder Zhou Enlai. While his political position can be attributed to this background, everyone knows that there was a vast difference between Li Peng and his adoptive father in terms of both ability and public image. Li Tieying, who was once secretary-general of the Secretariat, was the son of another elder, Li Weihan. Li Tieying, who once served as director of the Propaganda Department, later embraced more liberal views and opposed the "anti-bourgeois liberalization" movement initiated by the leftists. However, after the Tiananmen Square incident, Li Tieying, followed Jiang Zemin's lead and initiated a campaign to purge intellectuals, completely diverging from the path of his father. A blood relationship does not necessarily imply that there is an ideological inheritance. The saying "The father is a hero, and the son is a scoundrel" is an absurd notion that was used during the Cultural Revolution, but unfortunately it is now resurfacing.

To examine the question of "Who was Xi Jinping's father?" from the perspective of an ideological legacy, we must consider this both in terms of institution and in terms of philosophy.

From an institutional perspective, CCP political ethics have always placed party loyalty above all else. Beginning from the revolutionary period up through the Cultural Revolution, the ability to distinguish oneself from one's family members was a fundamental condition for CCP members. Xi Jinping is indeed the son of Xi Zhongxun, and this title did provide him with certain advantages, for example, allowing him to obtain a position in the Central Military Commission after graduating from university. However, today he is not in the Central Military Commission, he is general secretary of the entire CCP, representing and safeguarding the interests of the party. If he believes that the reform aligns with party's interests, then Xi Jinping can be considered a reformer. But if he believes that reform is threatening party rule, he becomes an opponent of reform. He undoubtedly knows that his father, Xi Zhongxun, opposed Deng Xiaoping's decision to open fire on the protesters during the 1989 pro-democracy movement. Xi Jinping is surely also well aware that his father's later depression and unhappiness that ultimately led to his death were primarily due to his differences with Deng Xiaoping over the handling of the Tiananmen Square incident. However, during his over ten years in power, has Xi Jinping shown even the slightest inclination to reexamine the Tiananmen Square incident? On the contrary, he has intensified repression of any commemorations or discussions related to the event. The reason is simple: he believes the student movement challenged the interests of the party. Yes, he is indeed Xi Zhongxun's son, but from this perspective, as general secretary, Xi Jinping is more a son of the party.

From a philosophical standpoint, Xi Jinping grew up in the 1950s during the period when the Chinese nation was dominated solely by Mao Zedong Thought. Descendants of the "red" families, such as Xi Jinping, naturally held Mao Zedong in high respect and the imprint left by Mao Zedong Thought is deeply embedded in their hearts. The Xi Jinping we see today, in both language and policy proposals, carries distinct Maoist colors. When he first came to power, during a visit to the National

Museum, he used the phrase "the road of rejuvenation is bumpy" to describe the situation in the Chinese nation at that time. He described the past of the Chinese nation, quoting Mao, as "The strong pass is a wall of iron is but an idle boast," meaning that China had suffered unusual hardship and sacrifice in the world's modern history, but today, again quoting Mao, he said "... man's world is mutable, seas become mulberry fields," referring to the country's hard-earned search for a correct road toward its rejuvenation, and tomorrow, then quoting the poet Li Bai, he said, "China will mount a long wind some day and break the heavy waves." That the first two are direct quotes from a poem by Mao Zedong indicates that Mao Thought is deeply ingrained in his mind and can be effortlessly recalled.

If he truly values the influence of his father, Xi Zhongxun, then Xi Jinping should also be aware that it was Mao Zedong's mistakes that led to his father's persecution and imprisonment, and that Mao Zedong's governing ideology was entirely incompatible with Xi Zhongxun's reformist ideas. If we consider the ideological legacies of Mao Zedong and those of Xi Zhongxun, to whose legacy did Xi Jinping turn? At least for now, it seems that he has chosen Mao Zedong. One of my friends in Beijing who is familiar with the members of the Crown Prince Party once told me that for those Crown Prince Party members, Mao Zedong is their collective spiritual father. From this perspective, Xi Jinping is very much the son of Mao Zedong Thought.

Yes, Xi Jinping is Xi Zhongxun's son. However, more importantly, he is a son of the party and a son of Mao Zedong Thought.

Question 12: What is the significance of Zhao Ziyang?

Part 1:

I once almost had an opportunity to meet Zhao Ziyang in person.

It was during the later stages of the June 4th movement, after Zhao Ziyang's speech on May 4th and after the imposition of martial law on May 19th. At the time, Zhao Ziyang had already been deprived of his decision-making power and was already under house arrest, but he was still observing developments in the square. One day, an elder who was a qigong practitioner went to visit him and then later found me at the place where our " Capital Joint Consultative Committee for People from All Walks of Life held our meetings. He informed me that Zhao had already lost his power. He suggested that I visit Zhao Ziyang at his home, and he said that he could arrange it.

At the time, I was in my twenties and I was relatively simple. Although the situation in the Square had escalated into a struggle for political power at the top levels, I still believed that I was participating in a student movement and that I should not become involved in upper-level political struggles. By the same token, the upper-level political struggles should not interfere with our student movement. At the beginning of the movement, some people offered to introduce me to Deng Xiaoping's children, but I refused because of this same concern. This time too I could not break free from my original thinking, so I ultimately declined the elder's suggestion and did not try to see Zhao Ziyang. Looking back now, I deeply regret it. This is not only because my meeting Zhao Ziyang would have had a positive impact on the June 4th movement (though at that time, Zhao was already powerless to change the course of events) but because I regret that I missed the opportunity to show my respect to him in person.

At the same time, I keenly felt that Zhao Ziyang, like many others in the history of the Chinese Communist Party (CCP), played the role of a tragic figure within the Communist system. From Chen Duxiu, the co-founder of the party, who was completely abandoned by the party, to Qu Qiubai, who was confused about his political choices before his death, to Liu Shaoqi, the president who had once been a fervent supporter of Mao Zedong but was ultimately persecuted to death, and to Huang Kecheng, who was disliked by the party's leftists for aways wearing glasses and who became a target of political struggles – the results of their political choices all turned out to be fatal mistakes. The ideals for which they had fought throughout their entire lives turned out to be monstrous deviations. When they woke up, they found it was too late, and they had become the very people whom they most despised and initially had sought to overthrow in the social revolution. Being consumed by the revolutionary monster that they themselves had created, what could be more tragic than this outcome?

After 1989, although Zhao Ziyang could already see the inherent resistance of the CCP to democracy, he had dedicated his entire life to this party, which ultimately deprived him of freedom and erased all his contributions to the party. What pains did Zhao Ziyang carry in his heart that outsiders could truly understand?

Zhao Ziyang has passed away, but as a political symbol, the existence of his name remains an opportunity for us to reexamine the true face of China today.

During the Zhao era, China's reforms were comprehensive. There were even discussions about political reforms. However, as the reforms progressed, they became limited to partial economic reforms. The problem arising from this was that although the economy was developing rapidly, China's politics, society, education, culture, and so forth, were not developing in parallel with the economy. This imbalance is the true face of China and the root of its instability today. Those who only view China from an economic perspective and believe that China can develop stably without political and social change have an extremely limited understanding. Therefore, Zhao Ziyang's passing represents the death of true reform in China. The current prosperity in China superficially conceals the essential underlying crisis, but how long this concealment can last is a question worth pondering.

Part 2:

I have never concealed my political stance of being anti-Communist. In fact, I find it rather strange not to be against communism. However, I also never deny everything the Communist Party has done just because of my anti-Communist stance nor do I discriminate against every Communist Party member just because of my overall anti-Communist views. I have always believed that as a party with more than ninety million members not every member can be evil, even though the party is an evil political party.

I have always believed that as a large party with more than 90 million members, it is naturally impossible for every member to be a bad person, even though this party is an evil political party. I believe that many CCP members are bad people; they join the party to gain wealth and power, and when in power they suppress the rights of the people. But they lack true loyalty and emotions toward the party to which they belong. Such members likely make up the majority within the CCP and this will ensure that the CCP will ultimately be eliminated by history because it lacks sincere believers.

However, I have never denied that among the more than 90 million CCP members, there are indeed some individuals with idealistic characteristics who are well aware of the flaws in today's political system. They join the party with the intention of doing meaningful things rather than wanting to become wrongdoers. While they may be limited in their capabilities, they try to do good within their capacities. Among them, there may even be individuals who genuinely want to bring about change: to change this party and to change the country. They might ultimately achieve very little, but that is due to circumstances beyond their control. One of the reasons for their helplessness and their inability to have any influence is that their numbers within the CCP are too few.

But no matter if others believe it or not, I believe that there are indeed such Communists. This is one of the many reasons I have full confidence that China will eventually move toward democratization. This is because as long as there are people like this within the CCP, one day, when the external pressures become strong enough, they will break away from the system, align with the outside forces for change, and change the course of China, much like Leon Trotsky did in his time.

This seemingly overly optimistic belief, but one that is actually supported by historical experience, is something I highly respect and admire in a CCP member. Moreover, he is not just an ordinary party member; he once held the prestigious position of general secretary of the CCP. That person is Mr. Zhao Ziyang.

It seems that this tragic hero of a generation seems to have disappeared from history, but there are still some aspects of him that grip our hearts. When looking back at the figure of Zhao Ziyang today, what I hope people will remember most is the life choices he made after losing power and freedom.

As we all know, after the crackdown on June 4th, Jiang Zemin took over the reins of power. He was a master of showmanship but he lacked any governing abilities, which led to Deng's Xiaoping's eventual dissatisfaction with him. During his

Southern Tour in 1992, Deng delivered a number of speeches, some of which were public and some of which remain secret to this day. He even mentioned Zhao Ziyang in these speeches, re-affirming Zhao's accomplishments and abilities during the 1980s. Deng publicly said, "Not a single word in the resolution of the Thirteenth Party Congress can be altered," indirectly expressing his approval of Zhao Ziyang because the resolution in which "not a single word can be altered" was drafted under Zhao Ziyang's supervision. At the time that Deng said this, Zhao had already been under house arrest for three years.

Another open secret is that after this incident, on two occasions Deng Xiaoping sent messengers to talk with Zhao Ziyang, telling him that as long as he admitted his mistake in supporting the students and then expressed support for the decision to suppress June 4th, he could return to the center of power, as chairman of the Chinese People's Political Consultative Conference or even as general secretary. This move was undoubtedly a political strategy on the part of Deng Xiaoping, hoping to shake Jiang Zemin's belief that he was irreplaceable and to make him pay heed to Deng Xiaoping's instructions.

At the time, Zhao Ziyang faced two choices: one was to abandon his conscience, regain power, and restore his freedom, which would also allow a way out for his family members to avoid being implicated. Of course, he himself could then also enjoy wealth and power. The other choice was to hold onto his conscience and refuse to admit any wrongdoing in opposing the suppression of the student movement. Zhao Ziyang chose the latter, telling the messengers from Deng that he would return to work only if the central government gave a correct explanation of June 4th . In other words, Zhao Ziyang stated clearly that he would not return to work unless there was a redress of the June 4th incident; otherwise he would not admit to any mistakes or return to work. He maintained this stance until his last moment, never wavering.

Anyone who understands China's reality should know how rare, difficult, and earth-shattering this choice must have been. How many people can resist the temptation to return to the pinnacle of power after they have already reached it? How many people are willing to give up their freedom as well as their children's happiness to adhere to their moral principles? There are many people in this world who claim they can do this, but very few actually can, especially among the Chinese. Yet, Zhao Ziyang did it. At the same time, I believe that with Zhao Ziyang's foresight, he was fully aware that history would eventually vindicate the June 4th movement. At that time, he will be recorded in history with honor. From this perspective, he was the most clear-headed individual within the Communist Party.

Zhao Ziyang was not a perfect person, and his method of governance had many problems. He was not even a proponent of democracy. However, at the most critical moment in his life, he upheld his bottom line as a human being, which was that he would rather forgo freedom and power than acquiesce, approve, or support a regime that used force against unarmed patriotic students. He was willing to give up fame and wealth rather than to betray his conscience. This is not an immensely lofty idea, but it represents the bottom line of human nature. Therefore, Zhao Ziyang's final choice radiates with the brilliance of humanity. This brilliance is enough to make me look up to him in awe.

Question 13: Why is it said that the Crown Prince Party is not a monolithic group?

Regardless of what people think about it, at least for a period in the future the Crown Prince Party, as a powerful faction within the Chinese Communist Party (CCP), will firmly hold party, government, and military power in China. China's future direction will largely depend on the decisions made by the members of this group. However, if we believe that a complete succession by the Crown Prince Party implies an unbreakable "red regime," we may be oversimplifying the situation. Looking back at the historical context in the development of the Crown Prince Party, we find that the Crown Prince Party is not at all a monolithic group and thus internal divisions will be inevitable.

In 1980, China carried out grassroots people's representative elections, and a group of "77" college students who entered university after the Cultural Revolution participated in the elections with the aim of promoting democracy. Among them were figures like Hu Ping, Wang Juntao, Zhang Wei, Fang Zhiyuan, Yuan Hongbing, Yang Baikui, Zhang Manling, and others, who later played significant roles in intellectual circles and social movements in the 1980s and 1990s. Some of those elected were also children of high-ranking officials who had been purged during the Cultural Revolution.

Liu Shaoqi's son, Liu Yuan, is now a senior military official with the rank of general and also a member of the top leadership group in the People's Liberation Army. He is a typical member of the Crown Prince Party. If we recall his speech during his election campaign in 1980, however, we will be quite surprised at what we find. He said:

During these past ten-plus years, together with the entire nation, I have experienced a terrible disaster. Four members of my family died and six were thrown into prison. Even though I can say that I suffered less than any one of the others in my family, I dare not even look back at my experiences; they were too horrifying. But what happened is deeply imprinted in my heart and I frequently think about it, allowing me no peace. I believe any child who has been forcibly separated from his/her parents would have similar feelings. I endured various insults and was thrown into prison several times, where my youth was buried. During days of extreme hunger, I lived like an orphan, or a wolf, hating the world. In those years, I was determined to survive. Who can witness their parents being humiliated and separated even on the execution ground, or see someone stuffing lit fireworks into the mouth of a nine-year-old sister? Can you imagine the pain in my heart? I gritted my teeth and endured it all. In my teenage years, I was subjected to labor reform under the whip, bleeding and suffering while in shackles. For many years, over thousands of days and nights, every hour, my heart bled and shed tears. Every moment, I endured inhumane treatment and pressure. But I refused to go mad. Why? It was to witness the day when truth triumphs over evil. Today, looking back at my past suffering, I will never allow others, or our future generations, to experience such pain! I must stand up and speak for the people. To avoid a repeat of the disaster, we must eradicate the soil that breeds feudal fascism and achieve democracy, no matter how difficult it may be, no matter how long the road is, from now on we must always strive for democracy.

The painful experience of the Cultural Revolution led some children of senior officials in the 1980s to show a relatively greater inclination to favor a democratic system. Liu Yuan is not the only such example. According to Wu Jiaxiang, who once worked in the CCP General Office, in about 1987 he came across a speech by, the daughter of Deng Xiaoping, Xiao Rong, who was then serving as deputy director of the Office of the Standing Committee of the National People's Congress. In her speech, Xiao Rong "fully affirmed the parliamentary system in developed Western countries, believing that some aspects could be used for reference in our country." Such members of the Crown Prince Party played a role during the ideological liberation movement of the early 1980s.

Now that the Crown Prince Party has taken full control of political power in China, the outside world inevitably speculates about their political ideas. Although we have a glimpse from looking back at Liu Yuan's speech during the 1980 election campaign, we do not know how such an inclination toward democracy during the 1980s and 1990s evolved. But at least from the perspective of its historical origins, some members of the Crown Prince Party did reflect about the CCP system. This group includes Luo Ruiqing's daughter Luo Dian, Chen Yi's son Chen Xiaolu, who also has publicly apologized for participating in beatings during the Cultural Revolution, and Hu Yaobang's son Hu Dehua, who has openly called for a reassessment of the Tiananmen Square incident.

Yet within the Crown Prince Party, there are others like Bo Xilai, who was willing to revive the specter of the Cultural Revolution to achieve personal power, and others like Chen Yuan, Wang Jun, and Kong Dan, who sought to control China's economic and financial lifelines. However, there are also individuals with a more sober and even a progressive perspective, such as Pan Yue in the past and Hu Deping and Chen Xiaolu now. In short, the Crown Prince Party is not a monolithic group.

Question 14: What are the political characteristics of the Crown Prince Party?

After the personnel changes made at the 18th National Party Congress in 2012, the unanimous outside view was that the Crown Prince Party was supported by the Jiang Zemin faction and it had emerged victorious over the Tuanpai faction. If this is the case,, the future Chinese political landscape will largely be under the control of the Crown Prince Party. Therefore, gaining a better understanding and analyzing the Crown Prince Party will help us assess possible future political developments in China.

In my opinion, as a distinct political faction, the Crown Prince Party has four significant political characteristics that make it vastly different from the Tuanpai faction.

First, the members of the Crown Prince Party seem to exhibit emotional and impulsive personalities. Bo Xilai is a typical example. In dealing with the issue of Gu Kailai, his wife, he acted impulsively and cast off Wang Lijun, who held a prominent position as vice mayor of the city, directly leading to Wang Lijun's escape to the U.S. consulate. This incident, which would never have occurred among the more cautious and composed members of the Tuanpai faction, was the direct trigger for the events that followed. "A small restraint prevents a great disaster," while a "lack of restraint" and an "unwillingness to restrain" are characteristic of many of the assertive Crown Prince Party members.

Even Xi Jinping, who seemed reserved and cautious in his early years, could not resist lecturing the United States during a visit to Latin America, saying "Don't speak ill of Chinese affairs." This undoubtedly reveals his inner thoughts, but it was probably a result of a momentary emotional impulse. It is difficult to imagine that such words would have come from the likes of Hu Jintao. But the group of Crown Prince Party members, due to their family backgrounds, are not overly concerned about the consequences of their actions, thus making them more prone to emotional outbursts.

Second, related to their emotional nature is the fact that many Crown Prince Party members tend to be highly individualistic. Although we can say that the members of the Tuanpai faction are relatively uniform, making it difficult to distinguish one from another, many members of the Crown Prince Party are easily recognizable and unafraid to stand out. Bo Xilai and Wang Qishan are prominent examples, as is Xi Jinping. During a recent media appearance, Xi Jinping spoke in a manner that completely deviated from the official tone, highlighting his individual character. If we compare the Tuanpai to a flock of sheep, the collective personality of the Crown Prince Party is more like that of pack of wolves, with their very pronounced individualistic characteristics.

Third, the Tuanpai faction is characterized by unity. It is rare to hear about members of the Tuanpai faction attacking or challenging their leaders. However, the same cannot be said for the Crown Prince Party. The serious divisions and disagreements within this party. Even before coming into power, had already seen events like Bo Xilai's flagrant open defiance of Xi Jinping. The incident reflects deep-seated divisions and conflicts within the Crown Prince Party. These divisions and disagreements are not merely due to differences in policies, lines, or personal styles. They are because the Crown Prince Party members carry long-standing factional conflicts and historical grudges resulting even from their fathers' involvement in earlier political struggles. For example, the four field armies formed during the Chinese Civil War led to internal divisions within the military, and these conflicts have been passed down to current power relations in Beijing. With the exception of Mao Zedong, all the other founding elders were essentially on an equal footing. Now, when some of their children are holding leadership positions, it is natural that there would be challenges from some of the others who refuse to accept their authority.

Fourth, many members of the Crown Prince Party experienced a fall from grace during the Cultural Revolution, tasted the bitterness of life, and lived as ordinary "people" for a time. This experience gives them a more populist inclination, making them more likely to use language that bridges the gap between themselves and the people. In other words, the "performative politics" of the Crown Prince Party is more pronounced compared to that of figures like Hu Jintao. Since Xi Jinping came to power, he has strongly promoted an anti-corruption atmosphere, which reflects his populist tendency to cater to public sentiment. His staged act of lining up to buy buns with the common person is a typical manifestation of the character of some members of the Crown Prince Party. In the future, we will likely see more moves by Crown Prince Party members to "get close to the people." However, this does not mean that they truly consider themselves on an equal footing with the people; they are at most populists, not democrats.

Personality determines destiny, and the political characteristics of the members of the Crown Prince Party make it difficult to deal with them. This will inevitably lead to a tumultuous and unpredictable political landscape in China's future, a landscape in which stability is unlikely to be the norm.

Question 15. What Does the Chinese Communist Party Most Fear?

Today's China exhibits some contradictory characteristics. On the one hand, the single-party dictatorship and totalitarian state control almost all aspects of society – from state-owned enterprises to local television stations – leaving no space for the development of any organized opposition. The ruling party also controls enormous wealth, a strong military force, and the public security and police systems. Its rule seems impregnable. But, on the other hand, one rarely can find any government or ruling party that is as fearful as the Chinese Communist Party (CCP). Few countries in the world, other than the People's Republic of China, require its citizens to go through security checks even to enter the subways. There is also no country in the world where surveillance cameras running facial recognition software permeate the entire society. And there is no country in the world where – when parliament is in session one finds security guards at every three steps and sentry posts at every five. The Chinese government's security measures far exceed those of either the U.S. or the UK, even though both the U.S. and the UK face an ongoing risk of a terrorist attack. It is no exaggeration to say that the Chinese regime sees enemies hiding behind every tree and is paranoid to the core.

This leads us to the following critical question: What is this powerful Chinese regime really so afraid of? I believe that the answer to this question has a fundamental significance for understanding the CCP.

First of all, we must realize that the CCP is not as secure and confident as the outside world imagines. The overbearing aggressiveness and insufferable arrogance of the regime are merely surface appearances. Deep in their hearts, the leaders of China who wield enormous power are full of anxiety and dread. It is critically important to realize this because it means that we should not be intimidated by the bluff and bluster of the CCP. Take as an example, mainland China's increasing intimidation of Taiwan. Many predict that the CCP will eventually use military force to invade Taiwan. But if you look at China today and think about how many resources are being expended to maintain domestic stability or how much military force is focused on Xinjiang, it is obvious that even if the CCP were intent on invading Taiwan, it would not have a sufficient military capacity to simultaneously support a war in Taiwan and, at the same time, to maintain the military strength it currently needs to meet its domestic and international security requirements.

Second, as is well known, it is exceedingly difficult to motivate the Chinese people to engage in collective resistance unless they are forced into a corner. Under the guiding governing principle of "nipping all turmoil in the bud," any threat of subversion to the CCP either from outside the country or from inside Chinese society really does not exist. There is even a clampdown on orderly civil society–initiated public protests, never mind any armed rebellion. According to reason, the CCP should not fear any threats from outside the country. But another possibility remains – there is a fear that comes from within. During a tour by CCP leader Xi Jinping, thousands of armed police were mobilized to protect him. Was he afraid that ordinary people might rush onto the streets to assassinate him? Of course not. What he really is worried about is assassination attempts by his political opponents within the CCP. The CCP is constantly on edge. This reveals one thing: the power struggle within the party is both brutal and harsh. This clearly cannot be denied. Otherwise how can we explain the pervasive and deep insecurity and fear on the part of this regime.

Third, and finally, perhaps there is yet another explanation for the Communist Party's frantic fears: the party itself does not know what it fears. As far as external threats are concerned, Chinese civil society does not have sufficient strength to successfully stage a revolt. From the perspective of a potential internal struggle, Xi Jinping's political enemies do not have any ability to turn the tide against him. But this regime continues to grow increasingly nervous. This may be because there is a permanent – if amorphous – sense of insecurity that pervades the system. The party has no confidence in the legitimacy of its rule and fears that the government does not have a solid foundation. It can be said that the party has a guilty conscience. If there were specific threats to focus upon and attempt to prevent, then perhaps the regime would not be as nervous as it appears to be now because it would know what it needs to deal with and what it needs to suppress. It is very likely that the regime knows that something will happen, but where, when, and what remain unknown. Facing an unknowable future causes the most fear. This also tells us something else: the CCP may face a political crisis at any time. This conclusion may sound sensational, but it can easily be explained by the CCP's extreme paranoia.

Question 16: Why does Xi Jinping remain on the throne?

Sometimes when observing the political situation in China, the more one ponders it, the more bewildering it becomes. Xi Jinping's strong grip on power is one such example.

Everyone knows that during the decade since Xi Jinping took power in 2012 , he has made a mess out of China and has created enemies on all sides. The economy is plummeting, the people have lost confidence in the government, and by normal standards Xi has no political achievements to speak of. When Xi Jinping first came to power, some people had high expectations and respect for him. But now, except for a few perhaps muddle-headed people, the vast majority of Chinese people are disgusted with him, but they dare not speak out against him. He has lost the popular support of the people, and even within the Chinese Communist Party (CCP), discontent with him is an open secret. From the members of the Crown Prince Party in Beijing to the regional bosses, from the Communist Party patriarchs to Premier Li Keqiang, Xi has offended almost every existing interest group. Even his past supporters – Wang Qishan, Liu He, etc. – after he assumed a third term in office at the Twentieth Party Congress in 2022 – all now remain silent. In other words, Xi seems to hold unparalleled power in the country and his consolidation of authority appears to be secure. It is paradoxical, indeed, but the reality in China is that a man so incompetent, crude, and unreasonable, who has enemies on all sides and is hated by everyone, is so secure in his power.

There are many explanations for this, such as his control over the military or his personnel decisions, but this is not the entire story. The most dangerous people are often his cronies, such as the Khrushchevs abroad and the Wang Dongxings at home. Human hearts are difficult to know, and people may be unreliable. Another theory is that the political factions are unable to reach agreement and cooperate with one another, so Xi Jinping is able to play them off against each other and defeat them one by one. Of course, there is also the problem of Chinese cowardice, that is, not daring to revolt or create a crisis for the CCP. So if there is no crisis, it is difficult to challenge the ruler. But I believe all of these factors are just drops in the bucket. The most important factor is structural; it is Xi Jinping's position as paramount leader, which is determined solely by the rigid CCP system.

Looking at China and the CCP through a modern lens is already a mistake. This is because China's political system is hardly modern, and to a large extent it retains the characteristics of a feudal imperial dictatorship. These characteristics include not only the fact that the emperor holds all power and is difficult to overthrow once he is enthroned but also, and most importantly, the emperor and state power are so interconnected. Xi Jinping often says: the people are state power, and state power is the people. Of course, he is talking nonsense. In fact, in China the leader of the Communist Party is state power and state power is the leader of the Communist Party. In other words, if the top leader of the CCP were to be overthrown, it implies that state power, not only one individual, would have been challenged. That is why most people in the Communist Party are unhappy with Xi Jinping but so few are willing to challenge him. Challenging Xi would be tantamount de facto challenging the single party dictatorship of the CCP. Those inside the system – no matter how much they dislike Xi Jinping – will not challenge the system because they are the system and they depend on the system for their survival.

After the end of the 1966-76 Cultural Revolution, from the masses to the old Communist Party cadres, there was a wellspring of anger against Chairman Mao who had initiated the ten-year disaster. At the 11th National Congress of the CCP in 1977, there was a mainstream demand for a complete negation of the Cultural Revolution and a swelling of criticism of Mao Zedong. Even Deng Xiaoping had suffered many political blows during the Cultural Revolution: he was purged three times and rehabilitated three times, and his eldest son, Deng Pufang, was persecuted to the point of attempting suicide by jumping from a building, leaving him a wheelchair-bound paraplegic for life. Deng Xiaoping could not in his heart of hearts have any love or respect for Mao Zedong. However, he still would not accept any criticism of the Chairman; he ordered that everyone look ahead instead of to the past. Mao's portrait still hangs on the rostrum in Tiananmen Square.

So why is the personality cult of Chairman Mao maintained to this day? This is because attacking Mao is tantamount to attacking the system. Deng Xiaoping had to rely on this system to remain in power just as the Communist Party must rely on the system to continue to rule China. The reason why Xi Jinping cannot fall is the same reason why Mao's portrait cannot be taken down from where it hangs above the Tiananmen Gate.

Some people may ask, then why were Communist Party leaders Hu Yaobang and Zhao Ziyang purged? Did Deng Xiaoping not fear shaking up the system at that time as well? That is because neither Hu nor Zhao were paramount leaders of the Communist Party. Although they had served as general secretary of the party, they basically were puppets of Deng Xiaoping. As long as Deng Xiaoping remained paramount leader, the purge of either Hu Yaobang or Zhao Ziyang would not threaten the survival of the system. But the case of Xi Jinping is different. He is now both general secretary and the paramount leader of the CCP, and there are no patriarchs sitting in the wings to keep him in check. In the tradition of the CCP, no matter how seriously Xi may mismanage or harm the nation, as long as he does not endanger rule by the party, there is no pressing reason to overthrow him.

Question 17: Why should we not pin our hopes on the rise of a Gorbachev in the Chinese Communist Party?

Initially, after the 18th National Congress of the Chinese Communist Party (CCP) when Xi Jinping rose to power, external evaluations of him were more positive than negative. Many liberal intellectuals were hopeful about the new leadership. Several prominent Chinese intellectuals even penned open letters, urging the authorities to pursue ambitious reforms, reminiscent of their expectations for the "Hu-Wen New Policy" during the previous leadership transition. Much of this hope was built on affirming the personal styles of the new leaders, like Xi Jinping, Li Keqiang, Wang Qishan, and Yu Zhengsheng, who were seen as departures from Hu Jintao's reserved and formal demeanor. They also displayed a willingness to use their own forms of expression and to reveal their personal styles. Wang Qishan recommending reading The Old Regime and the Revolution by Alexis de Tocqueville is but one example.

This hope was, in essence, a replica of the traditional Chinese political expectation for benevolent rulers or enlightened monarchs, whereby the fate of the nation is placed in the hands of certain individuals. It demonstrated a greater concern for individuals than for the institutional framework. However, it seems that many have forgotten that the era of strongman rule has passed, and the current figures in power are constrained by a number of factors, including the system itself.

Two examples illustrate how the current leaders are limited by the system: Hu Jintao and his close friend Wan Runnan, former chairman of the China International Trust and Investment Corporation (CITIC), studied together at Tsinghua University and once were very close. However, despite Hu Jintao's ten-year rule and his power to decide whether Wan Runnan could return to China for medical treatment, Wan has never been allowed to return. This indicates that even though Hu Jintao held significant power, he could not bend the system to his personal will. The other example is General Liu Yuan of the People's Liberation Army, who, as noted above, while studying in Beijing, participated in the 1980 democratic elections and vowed to promote democracy in China. However, after climbing the political ladder and gaining military power, he made no efforts to advance any political reforms.

We cannot say that Hu Jintao was completely devoid of humanity because a person entirely lacking in humanity would not have risen to such a prominent position. We also cannot claim that Liu Yuan's initial vow was a deliberate deception since many offspring of old cadres who experienced persecution during the Cultural Revolution share similar views. However, why couldn't they, despite their having achieved power, do something consistent with basic humanity and their original intentions?

This is because once someone joins the CCP, and especially its political mechanism, they cease to be independent individuals. They can no longer make political decisions based on personal emotions and personal beliefs because they have already become part of the system. In other words, when someone enters the system, they stop being just a person; they become the system or a representative of the system. The key criterion for the CCP's promotion and appointment of officials is whether such officials prioritize party loyalty over personal values. Figures like Hu Jintao and Liu Yuan were able to reach their current positions precisely because they passed the test of the system, that is, they showed their party loyalty. CCP political discipline dictates that party loyalty must always outweigh personal values. Party loyalty is crucial for the CCP to maintain its control over the country. History has shown that those who try to prioritize personal values over party loyalty in the CCP will be purged and will suffer dire consequences. Former general secretaries Hu Yaobang and Zhao Ziyang are typical examples.

Therefore, in my view, any expectations by the outside about leaders such as Xi Jinping are primarily rooted in an exploration of personal factors, such as Xi Zhongxun's influence over his son or the impact of the Cultural Revolution experiences of the Red Guard generation on leaders today. These factors do exist, but they cannot counterbalance the institutional system or the true nature of party loyalty. Given the long-established and entrenched rigid CCP political system, how can we place our hopes on individuals and expect a Chinese Gorbachev-like figure to emerge? This is a typical case of wishful thinking.

How to view the reality of China

Question 18: How should we evaluate China's reform and opening?

I.

In reviewing and reflecting on China's so-called "reform and opening" during the past forty years, we must first clarify two concepts:

First, when we are reviewing, are we talking about "reform" or about "economic reform"? If we are referring only to "economic reform," then we must acknowledge the rapid economic development that China has undergone during the past forty years, the significant improvements in people's living standards, and the substantial progress in building national infrastructure. In the field of "economic reform," the achievements are undeniable. However, if we are discussing "reform" as a whole, we need to understand that "reform" also involves comprehensive social and institutional adjustments. The economic aspect is only one part of the story. " Therefore, when evaluating "reform," we must comprehensively also consider political reform, social reform, cultural reform, and even reform of the education system reforms. If we only consider the economic reforms, any judgment we make will be incomplete and subjective. We cannot use merely the achievements of the economic reforms as the sole criterion to assess the entire forty years of Chinese reform.

Second, when we talk about "reform and opening," we must pay attention to the fact that "reform" and "opening" are two different things. Any evaluation of China's forty years of reform and opening depends on whether the emphasis is more on "reform" or more on "opening." In my view, China's development during the past forty years has mainly relied on "opening " as the fundamental approach to the so-called "reform." Internally, whether it was the household responsibility system or the establishment of a stock market, most policies focused on opening up to stimulate productivity. Externally, whether it was to attract foreign investment or to join the World Trade Organization, the primary goal was to open up the Chinese market to the outside world. Despite this, however, genuine and fundamental economic reforms have been lacking, which is one of the reasons why growth of the state-owned economy has been insufficient and economic growth has been heavily reliant on foreign investment and private enterprises. Such an approach of not touching the core of the old system but trying to drive economic growth by exploring new areas has led to a situation whereby economic growth is high, but the old contradictions remain unresolved, and new contradictions are continuing to emerge. As for the political and social aspects, there has been a lack of real reform, and even the opening has been difficult, as evidenced by the requirement of the International Olympic Committee that the media be open as a condition for hosting the Olympics. Hence, a characteristic of China's forty-year reform and opening has been more "opening " and less genuine "reform," or one might say it really reflects the true nature of China's distinctive reform and opening.

Only by clarifying these concepts can we make a more objective evaluation of China's forty years of development.

II.

Furthermore, we need to clarify the very concept of "reform" itself.

During the Mao era, the most sacred terms were "revolution" and "class struggle." In the Deng Xiaoping and post-Deng eras, "reform and opening" and "stability overriding everything" became the ideological foundation for Chinese Communist Party (CCP) rule. In particular, the word "reform" became the CCP's trump card; it not only was used as a banner to mobilize the Chinese population but also as a benchmark to seek international acclaim. However, is this so-called "reform" genuine reform? If we delve into the underlying meaning, there is much room for doubt.

The term "reform" itself does not inherently carry any sanctity or legitimacy. It only deserves the people's approval when it targets the backward elements and instead it aims to create correct and humane new things. "Reform" does not automatically lead in the right direction. For example, both

China and the United States currently call for a reform of the United Nations, but their interpretations of such a "reform" are clearly quite different.

After the Third Plenary Session of the 11th Central Committee of the CCP in 1978, reform and opening gradually became the most popular and most authoritative terms in China, thanks to the vigorous work by CCP leaders like Hu Yaobang, Zhao Ziyang, Xi Zhongxun, and Wan Li, who deeply recognized the mistakes of the Cultural Revolution. In the 1980s, the meaning of the term "reform" mainly represented positive factors, such as humanity, enlightenment, ideological liberation, and the elimination of past ills. It was also due to these leaders' outstanding work that "reform" received unanimous acclaim and support from people of all walks of life.

However, after the Tiananmen Square protests in 1989, the CCP, whose ideology was thoroughly bankrupt, still used the terminology of the 1980s but it secretly manipulated the actual meaning of these words. We all know that Deng Xiaoping once said that not even a single word in the political report of the 13th Party Congress of 1987 could be changed. However, looking back at this report, people would be amazed to realize how insincere the CCP had been about implementing political reforms in stark contrast to CCP commitments at that time.

Furthermore, the economic reform process has turned into a blatant form of primitive capital accumulation. Reform turned into a "magic trick" used by those in power to legally confiscate the state-owned property belonging to the whole nation and to transform it into the private property of various interest groups through capital redistribution.. If the reform of the 1980s mostly benefited the majority, the so-called "reform" today now seems to be a process of reclaiming interests. Under the illusion of prosperity driven by interest redistribution is the fact that the interests of the majority are being harmed. . No wonder some people say that "reform is dead" in China today.

The question is, if "reform is dead," what lies ahead? Is it "long live the revolution"? The truth will soon provide us with an answer.

III.

Looking back at the results of China's forty years of reform and opening, there are four characteristics that should not be ignored. These four characteristics have made China's path of reform and opening distinct from the development paths of other countries, giving rise to China's unique characteristics. Therefore, traditional development theories, such as the relationship between the middle class and democratization, are not applicable to the reality of China.

The first characteristic of the Chinese reforms is that China has achieved tremendous success in its reforms, especially in the economic field. However, these achievements cannot be solely attributed to the CCP regime. Society itself had accumulated immense energy, which erupted in the areas where the government relaxed its control, becoming a significant driving force behind China's rapid economic growth. International capital seeking markets for profit also played a crucial role in supporting China's economic growth. While completely denying the positive significance of the regime in the economic aspects of the reform might be extreme, we can at least say that the Chinese authorities faced a number of obstacles in China's economic development. These obstacles were particularly evident in their toleration of the dividing up of state-owned assets by elites, thereby exacerbating social injustices. As the reform slowed down and government corruption worsened, these obstacles became increasingly apparent.

At the same time, we need to note that, on the one hand, the scope of government power has been narrowing and the effectiveness and concentration of power are declining. In various areas and regions, such as in the rural areas or in the factories, incidents such as forced labor are occurring without restraint, while local and departmental interests are strengthening and solidifying. Nevertheless, the limitations on government power are also shrinking, the government's powers to mobilize are increasing, and even the concentration of power is intensifying. For example, each locality is under the rule of a single leader, which was not the case prior to the reforms. With a large amount of wealth at their disposal, the ability of these leaders to act has been significantly strengthened.

Similarly, on the one hand, there has been considerable progress in legal construction, both in legislation and in the judiciary, and the importance of legal procedures has been emphasized. However, on the other hand, the number of arbitrary actions by the government has also greatly increased. In practice, the government appears to be rule-abiding in daily matters, but at special moments, it can disregard or terminate enforcement of the law without restraint. These seemingly contradictory phenomena demonstrate the complexity of China's social transformation, which cannot be concealed by the economic prosperity or by the improved living standards.

Furthermore, when evaluating China's achievements in economic growth, we must recognize that this growth is actually supported by the political system of one-party rule, which significantly reduces the costs of reform and serves as the secret behind China's economic growth. However, this kind of growth is based on exploitation of the interests of the vulnerable social groups and is an unjust growth. Its costs are enormous, but they remain hidden when social contradictions are masked by the speed of the economic growth. Such economic growth only represents growth itself and does not necessarily translate into genuine social development. Therefore, it is a distorted form of growth.

The second characteristic of the Chinese reforms is that, in my opinion, the greatest crisis facing Chinese society today, after forty years of reform and opening, is the scarcity of a national spirit and the comprehensive decline of morality and ethics. The people's yearning for a national spirit is manifested in their defense of national unity and the high demand for national self-esteem as represented by events such as the Olympics. However, in contemporary China's distorted social environment, this budding national spirit has gradually been directed in a direction that opposes democracy, human rights, and other fundamental human values, giving rise to a violent form of nationalist fanaticism. This will be the most worrying social trend for the next decade. However, we should also recognize that as individuals are gaining more freedoms, their spirits are also growing. People are aware of the importance of their rights and understand that they need to defend their own interests. It can be said that in recent years high-profile political appeals for idealism have decreased and cooled down, but defense of one's individual rights and interests through realism is continuously gaining momentum.

The third characteristic of the Chinese reforms is that the wealth gap and social injustices in China have become increasingly severe. This is the result of the path chosen by China's forty years of reform and opening. From the beginning, China chose a path that encouraged a few to become rich first even though it created disparities in the system This approach has two problems: First, who gets to decide who gets rich first? In the initial stages of a market economy when it is not fully developed, it is evident that the market does not make such decisions, so it naturally falls to the political powers to redistribute wealth. Without a democratic system as a supervisory mechanism, this inevitably leads to social injustices. The vulnerable groups who have no connection to the ruling power become victims and, to some extent, they are mere stepping-stones for the interest groups to reap huge profits. But their discontent is accumulating and will eventually erupt. Second, as the market economy gradually matures and various systems take shape, the newly wealthy class will inevitably oppose further reforms in order to protect their own interests. They, that is, the privileged elite, will then become the biggest obstacle to future reforms. To some extent, this contradicts an important viewpoint in modernization theory, which is that a prosperous middle class will spontaneously drive democratization.

The fourth characteristic of the Chinese reforms is that, currently, although there are significant social inequalities, there are no signs of class struggle between the various social strata in China. Instead, the fundamental contradiction lies in the tensions between the government and the people. That is to say, political problems are increasingly becoming China's core problem. This will lead to three developmental directions: First, defense of one's own interests by the populace, leading to resentment against the government's arbitrary actions. Second, conflicts among interest groups, all of whom have the desire and the means to manipulate politics, thus necessitating the establishment of rules among them. Third, the disdain of the economic and social elites for autocratic power, with a powerful desire to limit this power. How these three directions will develop and evolve, especially in the absence of any control over power, will determine the political trajectory of China in the future.

To sum up, I suggest using a "state-society" model to

examine China's forty years of reform and opening. In other words, for China to change, it must adjust the relationship between the state and society.

We know that over the past seventy years, the design of the state system has been aimed at transforming society and individuals rather than making any adaptation to changes in the social environment. In a state-society relationship, the two sides are unequal, with the power of the state far exceeding that of society. To this day, such a situation has not fundamentally changed. Numerous social contradictions are, in fact, manifestations of the imbalances in state-society relations. Therefore, during the next ten years, one of the crucial indicators to observe in China will be the balance between state power and societal power. When a fully developed civil society begins to surpass the power of the state, it will mark the appearance of a "golden crossroads" – the starting point for China's genuine political transformation.

Will such a "golden crossroads" occur? I am optimistic. I believe that one of the outcomes of the forty years of reform and opening – an outcome not intentionally guided or desired by the government – has been the gradual growth of a civil society.

It can be expected that as the components of a civil society continue to grow, the level and extent of state control over society will be further weakened. As long as the decline of state power and growth of the power of civil society continue, such a "golden crossroads" will arrive. This will be the moment when China's democratic movement will begins to accelerate.

Question 19: Is China's economic development really successful?

I believe that while fully acknowledging the positives of China's economic growth, we must also recognize the four underlying costs of this economic growth:

•This economic growth is built upon social inequalities:

For example, the Gini coefficient in China was stable at around 0.16 from 1978 to 1984. However, it started to climb beginning in 1984, reaching 0.473 in 2007. A Gini coefficient below 0.2 indicates "high equality," while 0.2 to 0.4 represents "low inequality," and above 0.4 is considered "high inequality." According to data provided by Li Yang, vice president of the Chinese Academy of Social Sciences, the Gini coefficient reached 0.5 in 2009, and now it is estimated to be over 0.6.

Statistics from the Chinese Ministry of Finance regarding property income show that the wealthiest 10 percent of families own 45 percent of all urban property, while those families in the lowest 10 percentile own only 1.4 percent of the total property. According to a June 2010 World Bank report, 1 percent of households in China own 41.4 percent of the country's wealth, and the income gap between high-income senior executives of listed state-owned enterprises and the average wage in society is 128 times. The income disparities between the top 10 percent and the bottom 10 percent increased from 7.3 times in 1988 to 23 times in 2007. Thus, this economic growth is clearly built on an imbalanced foundation.

•This economic growth is built upon one-party rule:

The absence of labor unions as protectors of workers' interests is a major reason for the low labor costs in China. These low costs rely on the state machinery backed by state violence. This is the true mechanism behind China's economic growth. As Qin Hui has said, the characteristics of the Chinese model are "high growth, low human rights."

China's big domestic funds were instructed to subscribe to the Agricultural Bank of China (ABC) during its listing in July 2010, with some specifying that the subscription price could not be lower than 3 yuan. Fund managers indicated that the subscription quota and the share price would be taken into account in their annual performance assessments. The success of ABC's listing was thus crucial to the future of senior officials. This shows that, to some extent, China is still a planned economy, and political factors play a significant role.

Western judgments about the Chinese economy often forget to consider the political factors, which is the West's biggest misunderstanding about China.

•China's economic growth is built upon significant social costs:

According to a description in the Reader's Digest in August

2013, China is one of the world's most polluted countries, with all major rivers suffering from pollution, severe deforestation, desertification, and annual occurrences of droughts and floods. These are the costs of China's economic growth. According to a report by institutions such as the School of Environment at Renmin University of China, 9.567 percent of cities in China have good air quality, 75.8 percent have poor air quality, and 13.52 percent have extremely poor air quality.

In November 2009, Xinhua reported that there were about 170 million people suffering from mental illnesses in China and there were 16 million people who required treatment for mental illness. Another report, by China Central News Agency in September 2009, admitted that China has a high suicide rate. According to the China Center for Disease Control and Prevention, the suicide rate in China is 22.23 per 100,000 people, making suicide the fifth leading cause of death in China, with about 250,000 people dying from suicide and two million people attempting suicide every year.

Such a situation is the result of a reform that does not focus on national culture and spiritual levels and only focuses on economic growth as the sole direction of governance.

•This economic growth is built upon a rich-poor divide:

In 2008, China's fiscal revenue was 6.13 trillion yuan, an increase of 985 times over sixty years, and its foreign exchange reserves had increased by nearly 14,000 times. At the same time, after adjusting for price factors, per capita disposable income of urban residents only increased by 18.5 times over this period of sixty years. According to a report in issue no. 47 of Sanlian Life Weekly in 2012, the proportion of Chinese government spending on education, healthcare, and social security accounted for only 29.2 percent of total fiscal expenditures, which is half of such expenditures in the UK. Where did the money go? First, this is the is cost of maintaining stability, which now exceeds defense spending. Second, there has been large-scale infrastructure construction to promote economic development and to bring more tax revenue to the country. But has the country become stronger and have the people become happier?

When evaluating the success of a reform, we should not merely look at the output but we should also consider the costs. When the costs or prices are greater than the gained achievements, can such economic growth really be considered a successful model?

Question 20: If China's reform is described as a "disruptive reform," then who are the disrupters?

Several years ago, Professor Xiao Bin, vice dean of the School of Politics and Public Administration at Sun Yat-sen University in China, participated in a seminar at Taiwan's National Tsing Hua University's College of Humanities and Social Sciences. During the seminar, Prof. Xiao delivered a report on the development strategy of Guangdong province. In his report, he put forward an insightful idea. He believes that China's reform model can be called a "disruptive reform." This means that the initiation of reform in China often starts by tearing open a hole in a specific region or field. This hole then gradually expands and leads to a notable change in the overall situation.

Such a vivid description accurately illustrates the path of China's reform and opening over the past several decades. However, it is still uncertain whether this path will continue. Will China's reform and opening continue to proceed in such a "disruptive" manner?

In response to this viewpoint, I raised a question during the seminar: Who are the disrupters? I believe this question is crucial in determining whether China's "disruptive reform' and opening will continue.

In my view, after China officially launched the reform process in 1978, it has followed the basic path summarized by

Professor Xiao Bin – starting with localized breakthroughs, the so-called "disruptive" steps and beginning in specific regions, and then gradually extending to other areas and sectors. Some in China's academic circles have referred to this as the "forced mechanism" behind the reforms. This cautious and prudent reform path allowed the changes to take place under controlled conditions and thus they were able to achieve a certain degree of success.

However, the success of this reform path relies on the following prerequisite: the presence of "disrupters." Based on the experience of the 1980s, I believe that the key "disrupters" of the reform and opening during that time were the political leaders, Deng Xiaoping, Hu Yaobang, and Zhao Ziyang, who supported the reforms. In other words, without support from the central government, Deng Xiaoping's dominant position within the party, and strong support from figures such as Hu Yaobang, Zhao Ziyang, Wan Li, and Tian Jiyun in the Politburo, even with breakthrough reform attempts at the local levels, it would not have been possible to make any holes in the system.

Looking back, during the initial stages of the rural reforms, although there were provincial leaders like Wan Li and Zhao Ziyang who supported the experimental household contract responsibility system, and without Deng Xiaoping's support at the central level, the experiment would likely have been aborted. Many top Chinese Communist Party (CCP) leaders at that time, such as Wang Dongxing or Zhang Pinghua, were conservatives who opposed the rural reforms. The same occurred with the establishment of the special economic zones. Starting in 1982, high-ranking party officials like Chen Yun were skeptical and criticized the Shenzhen Special Economic Zone. Without Deng Xiaoping's support, even Hu Yaobang and Zhao Ziyang, who were in charge at the time , would have been unable to withstand such pressure and would have retreated. From the rural to the urban areas, the advance of a series of reform and opening measures in the 1980s would have been impossible without support from high-ranking CCP officials. Therefore, the true "disrupters" were the reformist leaders at the top of the Communist Party. Of course, this result was also a consequence of China's political system, which is fundamentally autocratic.

Up until today, China remains a one-party authoritarian political system, and the fundamental development strategies are still decided by the highest authorities in China. Since Xi Jinping came to power and taken over positions as head of the various leadership groups, the concentration of power has reached a peak since the founding of the People's Republic. Whether or not various "disruptive" reform attempts at the local levels and in different sectors can be promoted essentially depends on the attitudes of the authorities in Beijing. If Xi Jinping or those around him support such reforms, the hole for reform will be opened. If they oppose or do not support them, then local attempts will fizzle out. For example, there were attempts to implement local -level elections in places like Buyun Township in Sichuan, but they ultimately failed because they were not supported by the higher authorities.

During the seminar, Professor Xiao Bin also introduced the current reform of the social management system in Shunde, Guangdong. In terms of the specific content of the reform, it seems promising and aligns with the development direction of "small government, large society." However, despite Shunde's several years of reform efforts, why has the influence of this reform not expanded within Guangdong province? To a large extent, this depends on the attitude of the authorities in Beijing. The inability to promote this reform means that the Beijing authorities do not endorse this direction of reform. This is the crux of the problem in China today: we lack "disrupters" like Deng Xiaoping, Hu Yaobang, and Zhao Ziyang at the top who have a reform mindset and are willing to break through the old ideological framework.

Clearly, in a one-party authoritarian political system that remains unchallenged, any "disruptive" reform is always at the mercy of those in power and its prospects will always remain uncertain.

Question 21: What are the triangular power struggles in Chinese politics?

Beginning with the Opium Wars, it is said that China opened its doors and began its modernization process. By 1978, when China started its reform and opening, modernization had become an indisputable criterion for evaluating China's social development. It seemed that China had truly embarked on the path of building a modern and democratic nation, and it appeared that China had completely eliminated the characteristics of its feudal traditions that had persisted for thousands of years. However, this is a misunderstanding of China's current situation.

In my opinion, in certain respects of China's social development, especially in politics, the feudal characteristics are still very much pronounced. In other words, China's feudal imperial system still plays a role in politics today, especially since Xi Jinping came to power. Why do I say this?

As we know, in ancient times the imperial power did not represent the interests of the bureaucratic class. Various levels of bureaucrats were merely interest groups attached to the imperial power, who were seeking private gains. Simultaneously, the imperial power was not representative of the people's interests. The people were essentially slaves of the imperial family, and the role of the bureaucratic class in relation to imperial power was to manage the people on behalf of the monarchy. So, whom did the imperial power represent? It represented the imperial family or interests of the hereditary aristocratic group. Therefore, in feudal China, political development essentially consisted of a power struggle among three groups: the imperial power group, the bureaucratic group, and the people. When the bureaucratic group engaged in extortion and corruption, the people would resist, leading to the various peasant uprisings that took place during the various dynasties. Naturally, these uprising were not welcomed by the imperial family. Additionally, there were also conflicts and struggles that produced contradictions over interests between the bureaucratic group and the imperial family.

A new dynasty would emerge after a peasant uprising, and a new so-called aristocratic group, represented by a new emperor, would appear. At least nominally, this new aristocratic group taking power was to represent the interests of the people and to combat the corrupt bureaucrats to win the support of the people. In reality, this was also a process of redistributing wealth by seizing the assets of the bureaucratic group. However, after the new aristocratic group firmly established its rule, it still needed the assistance of the bureaucratic group to stabilize power and govern the people. As a result, imperial power and the bureaucracy would reconcile and jointly suppress the people until, one day, another uprising would occur, leading to a change in dynasties. This is, in broad strokes, the history of the development and succession of China's feudal dynasties.

The political situation in China today is largely the same: Xi Jinping, as a member of the "red second generation," exercises the authority of CCP rule, and he and the "princelings" are the members of a so-called hereditary aristocratic interest group. Meanwhile, other officials at various levels are typical bureaucratic groups. Their loyalty to the imperial power is not based on genuine devotion to a "true son of heaven" but rather on their privileged status to obtain wealth under the protection of the imperial power, i.e., through corruption. The problem is, just as during the feudal dynasties, if the corruption of the bureaucratic group becomes too serious, it will lead to uprisings. These uprisings not only threaten the lives of those in the bureaucracy but also undermine the foundation of the imperial power. Therefore, the new representatives of the imperial power, such as Xi Jinping, must crack down on the bureaucratic group to appease the people. As mentioned earlier, this crackdown on the bureaucratic group not only wins popular support but also allows the representatives of the imperial power to seize the interests of the bureaucratic group for themselves – a win-win situation. Rather than being an anti-corruption campaign, it is more like a redistribution of power and wealth.

The problem is, if this method of governance truly works, there would not have been so many regime changes in Chinese history. The repeated occurrence of such triangular power struggles indicates that this mechanism must have inherent problems and must unsustainable. For example, contradictions between the imperial power and the bureaucratic group will eventually erupt, providing the people with opportunities to resist. Such patterns have repeatedly occurred throughout Chinese history and will likely continue in the future.

Question 22: Who will cause the building to topple?

Among China watchers, there is overwhelming pessimism about the prospects for Chinese democratization. This pessimism is anchored in the argument that the Chinese people, accustomed to being enslaved, simply will not resist the autocratic system. Not only outsiders, but the Chinese people themselves, are quite discouraged about this destiny, as expressed in the saying "they lament their misfortune, but they do not rebel."

But this gloomy conclusion is incorrect. The error is evident in two respects. The first is historical nihilism, which disregards major events in Chinese history. Of course, there was no resistance when millions of people starved to death during the Great Famine (1958–1961). But there was large-scale opposition during the Xidan Democracy Wall (1978–1979) and the 1989 protests. Those who make nihilistic judgments are also making selective judgments, searching only for historical evidence that benefits them.

The other mistake is to only consider the big movements and to ignore the daily resistance, to ignore those small, even individual, daily protests at the grassroots levels. Those who make this mistake ought to take a look at the book by former Wall Street Journal Beijing correspondent Ian Johnson, Wild Grass: Three Stories of Change in Modern China (Pantheon, 2004; Chinese edition published by Gūsa, 2016). Three stories about people at the lowest rungs of society – a group of petitioners whose houses have been forcibly demolished; a bereaved woman who tries to find out why her elderly mother was beaten to death while in police custody; and a rights defense lawyer who takes the local government to court for extortionary taxes levied on villagers – demonstrate to the world the everyday bravery of ordinary Chinese. In China, writes Johnson, "… the push for change comes mostly from people we rarely hear of: the small-town lawyer who decides to sue the government, the architect who champions dispossessed homeowners, the woman who tries to expose police brutality. Some are motivated by narrow interests of family or village, others by idealism. All, successful or not, are sowing the seeds of change in China, helping to foment a slow-motion revolution."

Or take Wang Lixiong's political novel, The Ceremony, published in 2017 by Locus. In this allegorical prophesy, Wang takes the same stance as Johnson – resistance at the bottom rungs of society not only exists but will be a major variable in determining China's future. In the author's words, "All it takes is a self-interested bureaucrat, an ambitious businessman, a border policeman, and a politically ignorant engineer" to turn a seemingly iron-clad state to rubble. Wang's novel explores how this collapse would hypothetically unfold.

If you are still reluctant to believe Johnson's observations or Wang's predictions, you can turn your eyes to what occurred in Beijing when the city government moved to swiftly expel its so-called "low-end population." Many commentators assumed there would be no pushback. But on December 10 – International

Human Rights Day – we saw hundreds of "low-enders" take to the streets of Xuanwu, unfurling banners that proclaimed "protect our human rights"; we saw the police pursue artist Hua Yong as he took photos of the scene, and then more than 100 protesters who encircled him to keep him safe; we also saw the dozens of Tsinghua sociology undergraduates who documented the protests despite the threat to their own safety; and then we saw over 100 public intellectuals sign an open letter opposing the authorities' arbitrary actions. Does none of this count as resistance?

In reality, arguments that the Chinese people will not resist ignore a simple truth: just because the resistance fails, it does not mean that there has been no resistance. China has resistance. But it has not yet won.

Question 23: How should we view Chinese nationalism?

In 2018, the global relay of the Olympic torch for the Beijing Olympics sparked protests and demonstrations by Westerners supporting Tibet and by various human rights groups. At the same time, overseas Chinese, especially the student community, strongly supported and protected the torch relay, displaying a surge in nationalist fervor and attracting significant international attention. How we perceive Western concerns about human rights in China should also consider the question of how China should rise. Between the enthusiasm of the Chinese people for nationalism and the clash with Western universal values, I believe both sides should try to avoid a common misconception – that is, "confusing China with the Chinese Communist Party" (CCP).

Those in mainstream Western societies should first recognize that there are two distinct forms of Chinese nationalism. One is the patriotism promoted by the CCP, aimed at using nationalist sentiment among the public to legitimize its rule. The other is grassroots nationalism, particularly among the youth, which emerges organically as a collective psychology in the process of China's transition from a historically backward nation to a rising power. Chinese nationalist fervor and the CCP's patriotic propaganda may align on certain issues, such as the Olympics or sovereignty matters, but they can also conflict, for example, in attitudes toward Japan. Failure to distinguish these two forms of nationalism may oversimplify the current wave of

Chinese nationalism, potentially harming the feelings of the Chinese people while criticizing the authoritarian nature of the Chinese government. In the early 20th century, when Chinese intellectuals began to pursue universal values, the lack of respect for Chinese national sentiments by the Western powers led some intellectuals to turn to the Soviet Union. Both Western society and the Chinese intellectual community paid a heavy price. In the face of China's current rise, Western societies should learn from this historical lesson.

As for China's young intellectuals, they should be aware that China's rise in the international community will inevitably face unprecedented conflicts, including concerns and questions about the wave of Chinese nationalism. For China, this presents both challenges and opportunities. It is crucial to differentiate the policies of the CCP, especially in the political and cultural realms, which have not kept pace with the country's economic development. This is the main reason for Western concerns about China's rise. Therefore, the wariness of Western society toward China primarily lies in vigilance against the policies of the CCP, rather than enmity toward the Chinese people. The enthusiasm shown by Chinese students concerning the Tibet issue during the torch relay puzzled a well-known European left-wing intellectual known for his critique of mainstream Western capitalism. Such should not be viewed as Western discrimination against China. Instead, it should remind Chinese civil society that if China genuinely wants to rise, it will face demands from the international community for universal values. The real obstacle to reconciling these conflicting demands lies in the refusal of

China's current leaders to embrace political democratization. While we may be angered by the unfair reporting by Western media, we should also understand the importance of promoting political democratization along with China's rise. We must not abandon our pursuit of democracy and freedom just because nationalist fervor faces scrutiny from Western society or even lean toward defending the authoritarianism of the CCP.

About the Future of China

Question 24: Will the Ferguson prophecy come true?

The year 2009 marked the 30th anniversary of the fall of the Berlin Wall. Reflecting on the history of the collapse of the Soviet Union and the end of the Cold War is hair-raising because it all occurred so suddenly and unexpectedly. After the initial shock, many experts and scholars began to study the case of the former Soviet Union and to debate how such a large empire could collapse almost overnight. An analysis commemorating the fall of the Wall by Niall Ferguson, senior fellow at Stanford University's Hoover Institution. identifies seven key factors leading to the collapse of the Soviet-led socialist camp that began with the fall of the Berlin Wall in 1989. Based on these seven factors, Ferguson predicts that within the next two decades China's Great Firewall [of censorship] will collapse, just as the Berlin Wall collapsed. I call this the "Ferguson Prophecy."

Will Ferguson's prophecy really come true? Let's look at his seven major reasons for the collapse of the former Soviet Union and see whether they are consistent with China's current situation, and then make a general evaluation.

According to Ferguson's theory, the seven major causes

of the collapse of the socialist state represented by the former Soviet Union include: 1. Stagnant economic growth leading to an institutional breakdown. 2. A middle class that is not placated by empty political slogans, even if it is not expecting democracy. 3. Corruption, low productivity, and environmental degradation. 4. A regime, despite being propped by surveillance, which is lacking in popular legitimacy. 5. Everyone is accustomed to lying, making man-made disasters inevitable [e.g., China's Great Leap Forward famine]. 6. Border unrest – that will eventually lead to systemic collapse. 7. Finally, external forces promoting freedom such as those that facilitated the toppling of the Berlin Wall.

The first key factor exists in present-day China: China's stagnant economic growth is an undeniable fact. Given that there is a strict limit to how much economic stimulus can increase domestic demand, we cannot see any possibility of a revival of China's economic vitality. This situation has led to capital flight and signs of systemic breakdown.

The second key factor has a different manifestation in China: the middle class does not now necessarily have a desire for democracy, and for the time being, rule by the Chinese Communist Party (CCP) is accepted as necessary. Without a viable alternative, the middle class does not want to see political chaos. The middle class in China is much more conservative than its counterparts in the former Soviet Union and Eastern Europe in the late 1980s.

The third key factor is half-yes and half-no. Xi Jinping's anti-corruption campaign has been exposed as cynical and self-serving, and it is already recognized that the problem of corruption in China cannot be resolved. Another evil that the government itself recognizes is the inefficient economic development. However, it is important to note that the government attaches the highest priority to keeping China's social surveillance system efficient.

The fourth factor has not yet fully been realized in China at present. The digital totalitarianism of the CCP has surveillance technology that was unavailable to the former Soviet Union, and at least so far it has maintained Communist Party rule without being seriously challenged. The fifth factor is fully present. The Hong Kong problem is a good example. The Hong Kong District Council election results were unexpected by Beijing. This is largely due to the fact that the government departments in charge of reporting on Hong Kong and Macau only good report the good news and not the bad news. The probability of unexpected incidents caused by the layers and layers of lies is extremely high in China. Factor six basically accords with China's current situation. The reason for saying "basically accords" is that "border unrest" has already begun, but it has not yet developed enough to threaten the regime. But it can be expected that this border unrest will grow in the future. The last factor, the "external forces" that triggered the fall of the Berlin Wall also helped build Beijing's Great Firewall. But now the entire Western world has begun to reconsider its understanding of China, so it can be said that this factor is also taking shape and developing.

Summarizing the above analysis, of the seven key factors predicted by Ferguson, more than 70 percent are now present in China, so the fall of the system is very possible. But with 30 percent of the essential factors still not present, I have reservations about whether Ferguson's prophecy will be realized within the brief period of two decades.

Question 25: Is it wishful thinking that the Chinese Communist Party will learn from Russia's failures?

Since the start of the Russian invasion of Ukraine, I am afraid that the most important issue for people in Taiwan has not been the progress of that distant war but rather whether it will affect the situation in the Taiwan Strait. In other words, whether Russia's invasion of Ukraine will cause Xi Jinping and the Chinese Communist Party (CCP) to rethink the issue of unifying Taiwan by military force? In the United States, there is a similar ongoing debate, with many experts suggesting that China will be forced to postpone or even cancel its plan of a military solution to the Taiwan issue. At the recent annual "Two Sessions" of the National People's Congress and the Chinese People's Political Consultative Conference held in Beijing in 2022, the speeches on Taiwan appeared to be more restrained than in the past. It seems that Beijing has really learned a lesson from the Russian failure. However, I have a different view on this.

First, if one makes a rational judgment, the possibility of a Russian defeat in Ukraine is indeed reason enough for the CCP to rethink its option of attacking Taiwan by military force. If the Russian attack on Ukraine proves to be so unsuccessful, then from several perspectives – including the difficulties of fighting across the 100-mile-wide Taiwan Strait, the higher costs of the Western economic sanctions, and the impact on Xi Jinping's rule if such a war were to be lost – the Chinese side should give up its self-aggrandizing idea of reunifying Taiwan by force. However, external observers should not project their own mindsets onto the CCP and Xi Jinping and assume that the CCP and Xi Jinping will use normal rational thinking to make decisions. We should not expect rational decision-making from dictators and totalitarian regimes. If rational decisions can be made by dictators, then Putin would not have started the war against Ukraine. If rational decisions can be made, then the CCP would not have had to mobilize its army to slaughter unarmed students in its own capital in 1989. It is wishful thinking to hope that a totalitarian regime will think and act rationally.

Second, it is almost impossible for Xi Jinping to think about abandoning the idea of resolving the Taiwan issue. As we know, after taking control in 2012, Xi Jinping's absolute power has inflated his ambition to match that of Chairman Mao, as evidenced by his extension of his term of office as CCP leader by amending the Chinese Constitution. In order to maintain the comparison with Chairman Mao, Xi must deal with and resolve the Taiwan issue while he is in power. This is not only his personal "historical imperative," but also a necessary basis for him to maintain his rule. If he does not deal with and resolve the Taiwan issue, his legitimacy as leader will be challenged ever more fiercely within the Communist Party. In other words, if he does not address and resolve the Taiwan issue, the fact that he was able to renew his term of office for a third term will not be very significant. Some may say that because Xi Jinping was successfully able to renew his term of office, there is no need for him to take any unnecessary risk on the Taiwan issue, while others may suggest that his third term is a measure to avoid being purged politically after he steps down. Bot these arguments are wrong. On the contrary, if he fails to achieve anything significant during his third term, the possibility of a political purge will increase. To avoid such a scenario, taking risks on the Taiwan issue is Xi Jinping's way of remaining in power.

Finally, Russia's invasion of Ukraine will have disastrous economic costs, and it will turn back the clock on the country's development. It is impossible for the CCP not to see this and not to seek to reassess its capabilities. To a great extent, the results of such a reassessment may be unfavorable to China. But to think that the CCP will give up its intention to reunify Taiwan by force simply by predicting that a war with Taiwan might lead to China's economic collapse is a misunderstanding of the CCP. This Communist Party does not care about starving 30–40 million people to death for the sake of its utopian ideals, so why would it care about Western economic sanctions that would bring about the destruction of the people's livelihoods at home? It is true that the Western sanctions against Russia are very powerful, but if the CCP is forced to choose between "completing the great task of reunification" and "ensuring that the people's living standards do not fall," it will definitely choose the former. In other words, the CCP does not care about economic sanctions from the West as long as it achieves its political goals.

In short, dealing with and resolving the Taiwan issue was, is, and always will be an aspiration that the CCP cannot abandon. Taiwan should not have any illusions. The fundamental way to ensure Taiwan's security is to increase its military strength, prepare the entire population psychologically and increase the collective will of the people to resist aggression.

Question 26: Can we look at China based on the "Lessons of Putin"?

In April 2022, Russia was officially expelled from the United Nations Human Rights Council. This is one of the most powerful countermeasures by the international community against Putin's flagrant war of aggression against Ukraine, and it also dealt a heavy blow to Putin's personal reputation both internationally and within Russia. Putin of course has only himself to blame, but a brief review of Putin's rise and fall as political leader has some concrete lessons for China.

In the short span of a decade, Putin – who ascended to the leadership of Russia in 2000 – reached a breathtaking peak in his personal popularity. This occurred despite signs of political regression that gradually were being exposed, thanks to hi iron-fist crackdown on Chechnya, Russia's steady macroeconomic development driven by higher oil prices, as well as the "tough guy" image created by his Kremlin handlers through television. As Russia became one of the BRICs (Brazil, Russia, India, and China) emerging economies, the so-called Putin doctrine became a model for great power politics, and Russia became full of hope of "rebuilding the glory of the empire." Such a trajectory is in fact quite similar to China's model after Xi Jinping came to power in 2012.

The earliest reason for of Putin's decline from the peak was a series of large forest fires in 2010. In the face of that huge natural disaster, the incompetent governance by the Russian regime – which was masked by economic growth – was fully exposed and people's confidence in Putin began to crumble. People came to realize that although the government seemed to be big and powerful, whenever there was a serious crisis, it was not able to provide the basic services that the people needed. All the prosperity remained in Moscow, belonging only to the rich and powerful. Russia was a country with a polished exterior, shiny on the outside but corrupt on the inside. I think Shanghai – which has also experienced a humanitarian disaster – is a similar example.

Another key factor that has completely disillusioned the Russian middle class – which once firmly supported Putin – is that Putin, after becoming president and prime minister, did not hand over power to the younger Medvedev as expected, but instead chose to return to power. This incident has made many people – including many within the system who expected Russia to continue its Western-style reforms – feel that there was no hope for the future. The rise of an opposition on the streets – represented by Navalny (who is now in prison) –made Putin's golden era a thing of the past and his rule began facing increasing crises. This is also the reason why Putin took the risk of starting a foreign war as a last-ditch attempt to consolidate his rule.

Looking back at Putin's fall from peak to valley, we can see that although he really did once forge a glorious period for Russia, that glory was based on excessive debt and overdependence on an expanding economy. This led to excessive costs of governance and the resultant chronic fiscal deficit. Affording the excessive costs of governance could only be achieved if the economy continued to grow at a high rate, and once the economy slows and the bureaucracy is unwilling to make sacrifices, discontent both within and outside the system immediately began to erupt. In Russia, the issues of employment and social security, as well as the security of property, have become the focus of street protests. In short, the contradiction between limited financial resources and the high cost of governance represents a dead end for Putin's model. The failure to resolve this contradiction is the costly lesson Putin is learning today.

At the same time, we can also see that whether it is the attack against monopolistic interest groups during his early years of rule or the call to "rebuild the glory of the empire," whether it is the killing of the goose that lays the golden eggs strategy of economic development or the overdependence of the regime on economic stability, or whether it is the crisis caused by the incompetence of political governance in the face of sudden natural disasters – all of this not only occurred in Russia but also in China. Such an overlap of trajectories is not a historical coincidence, but the logical consistency between so-called "Putinism" and the so-called "Chinese model," an inevitable path of development resulting from a mix of authoritarian repression and personal ambition. In other words, the lessons of Putin today will certainly be repeated in China in the future.

Question 27: Will China replicate the Russian model?

A political joke that circulated in Russia in 2007 and a review of it today reveals a chilling degree of accuracy. The joke goes something like this: Putin and Medvedev were privately discussing a problem. Medvedev said: "We have to win the right to host the 2014 Winter Olympics. The economy is booming, oil prices are rising, your targeted poverty rate has dropped from 30 percent to 13 percent, and we even won the European Song Contest in your honor. Putin listened, nodded his head, and then declared that all this really meant was that they then had to win World War III."

This joke makes one tremble with fear because only 15 years later, Putin actually launched his invasion of Ukraine which may indeed trigger a World War III. Initially, it was just a joke, indicating that the Russian people at that time were aware of Putin's wild ambitions, but they did not think that he would really go so far as to go to war; otherwise, it would not have passed off as a joke. What the Russians did not dare to imagine at the time has become today's reality. Another interesting aspect of this joke is that if you replace the characters in the joke with a conversation between Xi Jinping and his cronies, and apply it to the political situation in China today, you will find that there is actually no inconsistency at all, and even the specific details such as the Winter Olympics and poverty eradication can be applied to the same joke in Russia in 2007 as it can be applied to China in 2022.

This, in fact, is an issue very much worth reflecting upon.

This political joke comes from the book Fragile Empire: How Russia Fell In and Out of Love with Vladimir Putin (Yale University Press, 2014) by Ben Judah, former Reuters correspondent in Moscow. I would recommend this book to all those who are interested in the development of Russia and China. Reading it today can provide us with a very important reminder: the development trajectory of China today is, to a large extent, a replication of the development trajectory of the Russian model after Putin came to power in 2000. In many respects, the degree of replication can be said to be slavish imitation, with little significant difference. If we agree on this, then we will have an important reference point for predicting China's future development path.

The book provides much evidence to support the above statement. For example, the author states: "In the 2000s, the Russian economy stabilized, and the increase in oil production and prices brought wealth to Russia. A new middle class emerged, Russia became a consumer society, and people traveled abroad in large numbers. Russians, who were becoming wealthier, lost interest in politics, and even rejected it. Putin's dictatorship seemed to be far away and irrelevant to them." I believe that it is not at all difficult to see that the overall state of social development in China today is almost exactly identical to that in in Russia in the 2000s.

More striking is to find that the "Wolf Warrior Diplomacy" did not originate in China, as the exact same phenomenon had already emerged in Russia several decades ago. From the perspective of foreign policy actors, economic self-confidence coincides with a change in self- perception. Moscow embraced the BRIC emerging economy label and began to see itself as an emerging power. Moscow's foreign policy discussions began to focus on anticipating a prolonged recession in the West and restoration of Russia's influence among the former Soviet states. Russian Foreign Minister Sergei Lavrov even noted that he believed the days of Western superiority were numbered. This is reminiscent of China's rhetoric in recent years about the "rising East and falling West," and the emergence of its so-called "Wolf Warrior Diplomacy." In an even more striking parallel, it was around the time when Russia began to become more assertive that "influential politicians began to ask Putin to 'follow U.S. President Franklin Delano Roosevelt's lead' and amend the constitution to run for a third term as president," and "Putin began to change."

Here we can see that the changes that have taken place in China since Xi Jinping came to power in 2012, as well as the changes that have taken place in Xi Jinping himself, are almost identical. Most importantly, the logic that led to such changes is also the same: economic growth boosts a ruler's confidence and confidence gives rise to an expansion of naked ambition, while at the same time the society ignores or tries to ignore political suppression because of economic stability. The final result is that, without realizing it, a globalizing society slowly regresses back to a monarchical model.

The similarity between the Russian and Chinese paths is obviously not a historical coincidence. Undoubtedly, there are many institutional factors that generate such logic. This, in itself, is a topic worthy of study. However, I would like to emphasize that a careful study of the developments and changes in Russia and Putin after the year 2000 will help us to understand and predict the past transformations and future direction of China and Xi Jinping.

Question 28: Why does faster economic growth lead to greater social instability?

After the fourth wave of democratization began in the Middle East, attention from around the world turned increasingly toward China's future development. There have been many discussions about whether the Jasmine Revolution that took place in other countries could also take place in China. Among the mainstream views is the belief that sustained economic growth in China serves as a fundamental guarantee for social stability. As long as a certain level of economic growth is maintained, large-scale social unrest is less likely to occur. The Chinese authorities share a similar perspective, making maintenance of a certain economic growth rate a fundamental policy. However, can economic growth bring about true social stability? The Jasmine Revolution in the Middle East provides us with the best evidence of an opposite perspective.

In countries like Egypt, Tunisia, and even under the authoritarian rule in Libya, economic growth in recent years has been among the highest in the Middle East. For example, Egypt's economy grew by 5.3 percent in 2018 as compared to that in the previous year, which is truly an impressive achievement. Despite this sustained economic growth, these Mideast countries experienced social revolutions that surprised many Western observers. The main reasons behind the social protests can be summed up in three points: unemployment, government corruption, and inflation. These three points are closely related to economic growth. In other words, the rigidity of the economic growth model leads to unemployment, the massive state-led infrastructure projects leave significant room for corruption, and such rapid economic growth is also a major cause of inflation. In sum, we find that economic growth, without corresponding reform measures, especially adjustments to the political system, may not only fail to bring stability but they also will contribute to unstable social factors.

Why is this the case? The reasoning is simple: when it comes to social stability, the key issues are not whether the economy is growing rapidly but rather, first, whether the benefits of economic growth are distributed fairly; second, whether the people are sharing in the fruits of this economic growth; and third, whether the people feel involved in the formulation and implementation of policies related to economic development. In other words, if economic growth comes at the cost of sacrificing justice, then this economic growth may become the root cause of social turmoil. The faster such economic growth, the higher the degree of social unrest. Participants in the Jasmine Revolution in the Middle East were not low-income households but rather representatives of the middle class and well-educated young people. Their discontent was not primarily due to an evaluation of the economic development itself, but rather mainly due to their pursuit of a fair opportunity to express their opinions in future social development.

Looking at China, have those who are obsessed with the high-speed economic growth considered that issues like unemployment, corruption, and inflation, which were fundamental factors triggering the Jasmine Revolution in the Middle East, are not only present in China but also are even more serious? Although China's economic growth has been rapid, the distribution of profits has been extremely unequal, coupled with the fact that the people have almost no right to participate in politics. In other words, social contradictions that can lead to revolution exist in China; this is an undeniable fact that exists during the process of continuous accumulation. We cannot determine when these accumulated contradictions will lead to social discontent and form a powerful mass movement. Nevertheless, one thing we can be sure of is that such a trend has already emerged, and various societal forces are pulling China in a certain direction. If this holds true, our conclusion is that the more China's economy grows, the more unstable Chinese society will become.

Guangdong is a prime example. Among the past incidents of safeguarding rights in Guangdong, the most notable were the rights protection activities of the villagers in Taishi Village and Dongzhou Village, along with the military and police crackdowns that followed. Even as the bloody atmosphere in Dongzhou Village had not yet dissipated, on January 14, 2006, there was another serious incident of a police crackdown on farmers seeking to protect their rights in Sanjiao Town, Zhongshan City, resulting in four to five dozen people being injured and one person killed. These three incidents share several common characteristics: the rights protection and protest activities were all partially or even entirely caused by land requisitions, and in their resistance the farmers demonstrated a very clear awareness of their rights and the government used a disproportionate amount of military and police forces to suppress them.

Analyzing these three rights-protection incidents that occurred in the southern province of Guangdong, we can draw one basic conclusion: against the backdrop of the current political and legal context, more rapid economic development may result in more significant infringements on the people's rights. Guangdong is not only located on the coast but it is also adjacent to Hong Kong, which is a gateway for attracting investment. The degree of economic openness in Guangdong has always been at the forefront. However, as we saw in the compensation for land requisitions in Sanjiao Town, the town government sold the land to Hong Kong businesspeople at a price of tens of thousands of yuan per mu, but only offered the farmers, who made their living by farming, a few thousand yuan per mu. This kind of economic development not only failed to bring real benefits to the majority of people but also pushed them in the direction of even more dire circumstances.

China's land requisition process is not a transaction between two equal economic entities but rather a process of unilateral decision-making and pricing process of encroachment. According to China's relevant regulations, the property rights to land used for agricultural production and livelihood belong to an abstract collective. However, when collective land is converted into industrial land, a series of complex procedures and word games occur. After this convoluted process, the land price increases several times over or even tens of times. The appreciated portion is taken by various inefficient, bloated, and corrupt institutions, part of it is usurped by parties involved in collusion with officials and businesspeople, and then a portion is plundered by greedy local officials. Finally, the compensation to the farmers is merely a symbolic consolation.

The problem is this: land is the lifeblood of the farmers. If you requisition their land without providing sufficient compensation, how can the displaced farmers face the future? Of course, the massive Chinese system has never lacked beautiful promises and lies. Still, in today's society where people are becoming increasingly aware and information is circulating rapidly, the power of lies is losing its effect, especially in places like Guangdong, which is close to Hong Kong where people have more channels to obtain information. As a result, resistance is becoming more determined and straightforward.

Thus, other than deploying the military and police, there really is no way for the thoroughly corrupt system and the greedy local officials to continue their plunder and encroachment. Unless the Chinese Communist Party (CCP), officials are willing to be prepared psychologically to suppress resistance to the end.

Guangdong is China's most economically developed province. At the beginning of the reform and opening period, people could generally share the benefits brought by economic growth. However, due to the backward political concepts, the privileged capitalists harbored an end-of-the-world complex and became increasingly unscrupulous in the division and encroachment of wealth. The farmers who lost their land near the city no longer have the same opportunities for prosperity as they did in the 1980s through development. Instead, what economic development brings them is often poverty, environmental pollution, worsening public security, and so forth. The land left by their ancestors is taken away by the current generations. Furthermore, under sustained inflation, the wages of manual laborers in Guangdong province have remained unchanged for more than ten years. More than a decade ago, general laborers in Guangdong's factories could earn about 500 yuan per month, but this has not changed to this day. This makes it almost impossible for the farmers who have lost their land to improve their lives. What else can they do other than resist?

We should remind the Chinese people and international observers who have unrealistic fantasies about China's economic development that under the current political situation in China, economic development may not necessarily bring civilization and prosperity. This pathological economic development may well become an excuse for plunder. As economic development continues, social contradictions are accumulating , which may become the root cause of future social unrest.

Question 29: Why do Chinese people remain silent?

When discussing the current political reality in China, it is widely known that there is widespread dissatisfaction with Chinese Communist Party (CCP) rule . This is evident as the authorities treat any dissenting voices as a severe threat, indicating the authorities' awareness of the prevalence and seriousness of dissatisfaction. They fear that any sudden event could trigger widespread discontent. However, it should also be acknowledged that in Chinese public life, despite the widespread internal dissatisfaction, there is limited public expression of discontent. This creates a false impression to the outside world that general satisfaction with the government is relatively high. Many naive Western media outlets and deliberately ignorant Taiwanese media report on China in such a manner. The question is, why do so many Chinese people feel dissatisfied, yet so few openly express their discontent?

Fear is undoubtedly a fundamental reason. The authorities exert great pressure through strict control over freedom of speech. Publicly expressing dissatisfaction or protesting can lead to being monitored by the authorities or even being arrested. In such a political environment, few possess the courage it takes to openly express discontent. Criticizing Chinese people for not daring to resist shows a lack of empathy. Put yourself in their shoes and consider whether you would be willing to speak up in a society where telling the truth could cost you your freedom.

However, if fear is the only reason Chinese people are not

speaking out, then we are oversimplifying the issue. Following this logic, tyranny will never end because oppressive regimes will always create fear to maintain in power. Oppressive rule cannot persist forever because silence is not caused solely by fear.

In China, there are few public expressions of discontent with the political reality for several reasons:

First, it must be acknowledged that there are limited voices of dissent because there are still many people who are genuinely satisfied with CCP rule and China's current realities. This includes not only the ruling elites but also members of powerful interest groups who are satisfied with how their living standards have improved, even if they do not place a priority on democratic values. Ignoring the fact that there are people satisfied with CCP rule would be shortsighted. It is essential to recognize that the CCP does have its supporters, and even if China were to democratize, some would still support the party, much as the Guomindang still has supporters in Taiwan today.

Second, some people do not publicly express their dissatisfaction publicly out of helplessness. While they may have inner dissatisfaction and be aware of the government's actions, they cannot see how openly expressing their discontent could bring about any change. They feel uncertain about what they can do and they do not see any alternative power that could replace the CCP. They feel disappointed, or even desperate, about this reality, which leads them to keep their dissatisfaction to themselves. This silence can also be seen as a form of protest or an expression of discontent. It is essential to consider the proportion of people who refuse to participate in surveys, as it also can reflect the level of dissatisfaction.

Third, some people gradually adapt to the situation. They are not satisfied with the reality, nor are they oblivious to China's many problems. However, they have become desensitized about the unsatisfactory state of affairs, much like the story of the frog in boiling water that becomes accustomed to the heat. They consider this environment to be normal and natural. Since they have adapted, they see no reason to openly express their dissatisfaction. It is important to note that Chinese people have a strong tolerance for enduring challenging situations.

Last, some people choose not to express dissatisfaction openly due to their indifference. Every society has individuals who lack enthusiasm for the world around them and have little interest in social engagement or public affairs. They only care about trivial matters. For example, many from the post-1990 generation are more interested in anime and video games than they are in public affairs. Such individuals exist in democratic societies as well, let alone in non-democratic societies like China where they are even more prevalent. This large group of indifferent individuals contribute to the reduced number of people willing to express their discontent.

In summary, although a sizable portion of Chinese people are dissatisfied with the CCP, most are not willing to express their discontent openly either due to fear, satisfaction, helplessness, adaptation, or indifference. Surface-level satisfaction with the regime in China is not genuine or heartfelt. Whether it is fear, helplessness, adaptation, or indifference, these attitudes are highly variable and can shift overnight if the external societal conditions change. The fall of the Soviet Communist Party and the former Communist regimes in Eastern Europe in 1989 serve as precedents. Some may not understand this, but the CCP understands it quite well. That is why, despite the global perception of its strong grip on power, the CCP remains always vigilant and fearful of its own people.

Question 30: Why can Chinese people tolerate smog?

Behind China's rapid economic development lies unbridled environmental destruction, the most prominent manifestation of which is smog. Regardless of how some nationalist individuals take pride in China's achievements, the mention of smog leaves most people speechless. Smog in China has moved from being merely an economic issue to being a political problem, vividly highlighting the internal flaws of the Chinese model and displaying the negative side of the CCP's governance capacity. Even more concerning is the fact that the widespread smog across China now threatens the health of the people, especially the children.

It is natural for Chinese citizens to feel dissatisfied as the smog directly affects their well-being. However, this discontent usually finds expression through online grievances and in personal conversations but it seldom is transformed into large-scale protests or social unrest. Citizens may be indifferent or reluctant to publicly express their views on national issues, but why does such a serious issue like smog, which affects their own and their children's health, not triggered social instability? What kind of societal mindset allows Chinese people to endure such severe smog? And how does this societal mindset impact China's social and political transformation?

In a letter to the editor published in the January issue of Sanlian Life Weekly, the author, identifying himself as "a reader from Harbin" expressed his thoughts about the smog: "In this polluted air, even gasping for breath becomes difficult, and life feels like a struggle crawling within a cage. While the country pursues economic development and the rich desire ever more wealth, most people can only think: 'I Can't even afford a house, so what is the use of dignity?' Although the environmental conditions in the big cities is serious, people still keep migrating to the big cities, and those who remain in the big cities do not want to leave. Thus, there have been no major gatherings, no mass protests, and no nationwide mobilization. When people hear that there will be smog the next day, they merely think to themselves: 'Oh, I understand.' The only thing that might stir people's anger is the ridiculous words from certain experts. Smog has persisted for so long that people have become accustomed to it. Online, you can even find some humorous rhymes or witty remarks, especially from people in central and western China, where such humor seems a bit awkward when poking fun at something that harms their own lives. But perhaps it is their way of expressing their powerlessness. In my view, this represents a straightforward and typical reaction to the smog among many people.

Undoubtedly, most people feel extremely dissatisfied about the smog, and the phrase "struggle within a cage" carries significant weight, reflecting strong emotions. Such sentiments are widespread. However, first of all, although the smog is severe, many people are confronting even more pressing survival issues, such as work and housing issues. Beijing, despite being heavily affected by smog, still sees a large influx of people from other regions. Rarely do we witness Beijing residents relocating to other provinces due to the smog. This is mainly because the city offers more job opportunities, making urban life there more attractive. For many, the ability to afford housing today takes precedence over the damage to one's health caused by the smog tomorrow – future concerns are often overshadowed by immediate needs.

Second, no matter how dissatisfied people may be with the serious social problems, if the problems persist for a long time, they tend to become desensitized to them. In China, the sense of helplessness toward the government exacerbates this situation.

Third, although the CCP tightly controls the internet, it has not yet reached the point of entirely banning expressions of discontent on the internet, especially on non-political issues like smog. This allows Chinese people to freely vent their emotions through ridicule or even engaging in "self-mockery." When inner dissatisfaction is expressed through various "jokes," it offers some relief without building up into large-scale protests. Internet freedom can sometimes serve as a tool for the ruling authorities to maintain social stability. This paradox is especially evident in China.

The above letter from a reader represents the sentiments of ordinary citizens and reflects a part of the broader picture in China. Although the tone is flat, it provides insight into why China continues to develop in its current state.

Question 31: Why Should We Read People's Daily to Understand Chinese Politics?

Do not think I am joking when I say this. It is actually true.

Of course, there are numerous publications, especially from Hong Kong, and rumors on the internet about the upper echelons of Chinese political elites – the power struggles, factional battles, scandals of high-ranking officials, and rampant corruption. One might think that information is abundant. So why bother reading, People's Daily, the official mouthpiece of the Chinese Communist Party (CCP)?

The reason is that none of the information provided in those outlets mentioned above about Chinese politics is not very reliable. First, it is challenging to distinguish between truth and falsehood. Not all reports are false, as some may be proven to be true at a later date. However, many publications and internet rumors have turned out to be baseless. How can we discern what is true and what is false? It is almost impossible. If we could easily distinguish between the rumors and the truth, then we would not need to read those rumors in the first place.

Second, the CCP's official propaganda system has long been aware of the importance of spreading politically advantageous rumors by "exporting them for internal consumption." Different factions within the CCP occasionally feed certain media outlets with true or false information to serve their own political objectives. How can information about Chinese politics obtained through such methods be considered reliable? The likelihood of being deceived is significant.

Some readers might argue, "So, is People's Daily trustworthy? Isn't it full of lies?" It is true; People's Daily is indeed filled with lies to the point that during the student movement, the slogan "People's Daily speaks nonsense" was chanted. There is a popular joke in China that says that there is nothing truthful in People's Daily except the date (meaning even the weather forecast cannot be trusted). I fully acknowledge all of this. Then why do I still suggest that if you want to understand the real state of Chinese politics, you should also read People's Daily?

The rationale is straightforward. First, People's Daily is, after all, China's most authoritative official media. CCP decisions and documents published in People's Daily usually have been vetted and approved by the Central Propaganda Department or even by the Politburo before they are released. Therefore, People's Daily is the most authoritative and reliable source for to analyze CCP political trends. For example, whenever rumors spread about the CCP "reexamining the June 4th incident," I always say I won't believe it unless People's Daily publishes a resolution on the front page officially reassessing the movement The fact is that People's Daily has never published such a decision, and there has been no reversal of the verdict on the June 4th incident.

Second, although People's Daily is indeed full of lies, lies also have an analytical value, especially when one is dealing with a party and government that habitually lie. Such lies become even more valuable analytically. I suggest reading People's Daily, not to believe what it says, but to analyze the truth behind its lies. In other words, you need to learn how to read People's Daily from a negative perspective. By doing so, you might discover many interesting things. For instance, when People's Daily talks about "building a harmonious society," we all know that China's society is really far from harmonious (otherwise, why mention it?). When People's Daily stresses "resolutely upholding the party Central Committee with Comrade Xi Jinping at the core," we know that there are people who do not support the "party Central Committee with Comrade Xi Jinping at the core" (otherwise, it would just be stating the obvious).

Those who truly understand Chinese politics are those who read and comprehend People's Daily. The focus is not on People's Daily per se, but rather on whether you read it and can understand its implications.

Question 32: Is the people's distrust of the government the biggest hidden concern of the Chinese Communist Party?

The 1989 Tiananmen Square democracy movement in China is now 34 years in the past. When reflecting on and reviewing that movement, one point that is often mentioned is that the protesters at the time trusted the government too much and did not believe that the government would actually open fire on the people. This led to the bloody suppression by the Chinese Communist Party (CCP), catching the unprepared protesters off-guard. Such a reflection indicates indirectly that in the 1980s, there was still some trust in the Chinese government among the people (although it proved to be misplaced). In Chinese society today, although there is a certain amount of discontent, we rarely see protests in the major cities. This is a result of learning from experience. The people no longer believe that the government will respond kindly to their protests; they know that taking to the streets will likely lead to another bloody crackdown. In other words, compared to the situation in the 1980s, the people no longer have trust in the government.

This lack of trust is not only evident in the political sphere but also in various aspects of daily life. Let me give an example: According to a report in China's Economy and Finance magazine, a few years ago, the International Brand Center under China's Ministry of Commerce began planning to "resell" surplus products meant for Hong Kong back to mainland China.

The first batch of bids for this 20 billion yuan worth of fresh products, including meat, poultry, eggs, dairy, fruits, vegetables, rice, flour, oil, and seasonings, which were originally supplied from China to Hong Kong, will now be sold in trial cities such as Beijing, Shanghai, Shenzhen, the Yangtze River Delta, and the Pearl River Delta.

To those unfamiliar with China, this news might seem perplexing: why would products supplied from China to Hong Kong need to be "resold" back to the mainland? Wouldn't this double the transportation costs? However, those who understand China's economic and social development can probably figure out the reason: it is due to the people's lack of trust in the government. Why is this the case? In fact, there has been a fifty-eight-year history of supplying goods from mainland China to Hong Kong, and these goods are high quality because they are specially supplied. When it comes to fresh food, the safety and quality rate reaches 99.9 percent.

However, as is widely known, mainland China has serious food safety issues, and reports of consumers going to Hong Kong or overseas to purchase items such as milk powder are not unheard of. The key here is the issue of regulation of food production. On the surface, some of mainland China's food safety standards are not inferior to those in Hong Kong. For example, Hong Kong's standard for preserved meat allows nitrite levels of no more than 200 ppm, while the requirement on the mainland is no more than 30 ppm. It seems that the mainland's standard is much higher than that for products destined for Hong Kong, but why do people still prefer the products supplied to Hong Kong? This is clearly a matter of trust. Many Chinese people do not trust the regulatory efforts by the relevant departments in mainland China. Even if there are high standards, most people do not believe that these standards are being enforced. Liu Yuanju, a researcher at the Shanghai Institute of Finance and Law, has noted:, "Food regulation is just a small system. Behind it, there is a big system as well as support for cultural customs. Strengthening regulation seems easy, but it requires a clean government, public officials who are strictly supervised, transparent information, a free media, rule-conscious enterprises and employees, and so forth. These factors are not lacking in Hong Kong, but in the mainland progress is still needed." This analysis hits the nail on the head in explaining why fresh food products that were originally transported from mainland China to Hong Kong are now being "resold" back to the mainland. Ultimately, the reason is the lack of trust the Chinese people have in their own government and its officials.

Since taking office, Xi Jinping has consistently emphasized the need to strengthen the country's governing capacity. However, in a country filled with various social contradictions, if the people generally have a collective mindset of distrust toward the government, then when faced with a major crisis, such as an economic crisis, the country will have difficulties in governing unless it resorts to methods such as the state violence employed during the bloody crackdown on the June 4th incident in 1989. This presents the CCP with the biggest hidden problem that it faces in ruling the country.

Question 33: How do you view the "Little Pink" phenomenon?

In recent years, the "Little Pink" phenomenon has become popular among the younger generations in China, and it seems to be growing stronger by the day. Regardless of how incomprehensible it may seem to the outside world, there is indeed a significant number of members of the post-'90s and post-'00s generations who support the ruling Chinese Communist Party (CCP) and are satisfied with the current state of affairs in China. They do not discern right from wrong and they attribute all of China's problems to "hostile foreign forces," often indicating their narrow nationalism. The emergence of such a generation is certainly not something we welcome, as it hinders the progress of civilization in Chinese society today. However, merely blaming or looking down on the members of these generations will not help. Instead, we should strive to understand them and view the "Little Pink" phenomenon correctly.

First and foremost, we need to understand the reasons behind the formation of the "Little Pink" phenomenon. This young generation did not experience the Cultural Revolution or the June 4th incident. Using the current popular saying, they have not "tasted the iron fist of socialism." Instead, from birth to adulthood, they have only witnessed the apparent prosperity brought about by China's economic growth. Due to their limited life experiences and the lack of freedom of speech in China, they cannot see the darkness and the costs beneath the surface prosperity. Consequently, they wholeheartedly believe that Chinese society is progressing and that governance by the Chinese Communist Party (CCP) is commendable. To some extent, this perspective is understandable. However, I believe that as they grow older and their exposure to society broadens, their views will gradually change. The post-'80s generation also went through a "pink" phase, but now that they are already in their thirties, their overall "pinkness" has significantly diminished. Such changes can also be expected among the members of the current "Little Pink" generation as they mature.

Second, we must recognize that today's "Little Pink" phenomenon is, to a large extent, a result of manipulation and facilitation by the CCP authorities. In China, fluctuations in nationalist sentiments are entirely under the control of the CCP. Without the permission and support of the Communist Party, there would be no room for the proliferation of expressions of nationalist emotions. For a long time, the CCP relied on economic growth and nationalism as the pillars to support its rule. Now that the economic growth pillar is shaking, the party must exert greater efforts to uphold and strengthen the pillar of nationalism. In recent years, China's "wolf warrior diplomacy" that has become popular has shocked the outside world. However, the underlying logic is clear: with stagnating economic growth, nationalism becomes even more critical for the survival of the CCP. In this context, the party has intensified its guidance of the "Little Pink" phenomenon among the younger generation, and organizations like the Communist Youth League make various propaganda efforts online . Therefore, the "Little Pink" phenomenon is not simply a characteristic of China's young generations but rather it reflects the crisis that CCP rule is facing and the adaptive measures it is taking to respond to that crisis. The emergence and intensification of the "Little Pink" phenomenon are the results of the Communist Party's efforts to cope with the crisis.

Finally, however, there is no need to overly exaggerate the "Little Pink" phenomenon among China's young generation. In today's China, where freedom of speech is restricted, it is highly debatable how many and how influential the "Little Pink" individuals are. Their strong voice is partly due to their adept use of the internet, which allows their actions and opinions to be more visible. However, as they gradually step out of the shelter of their families and face life's pressures, it is doubtful whether they will be able to continue to maintain their confidence in the CCP. Even the most fervent "Little Pink" supporters will not genuinely reject the material consumption of Western capitalism. Based on this, their "pink" enthusiasm may not extend far in their lives. In other words, the "Little Pink" generation is changing rapidly, and the CCP must constantly brainwash the next generations to maintain its large army of "Little Pinks." This will not be an easy task.

Question 34: Could China have turned out differently from what it is today?

Today's China presents its own unique characteristics, under names like the "Chinese model" and the "Chinese path" that prioritize "maintaining stability at all costs" and "developing the economy at all costs." While "maintaining stability" and "economic development" may sound like reasonable policy objectives, the underlying premise of "at all costs" has led China down a path of political repression, veering dangerously toward a regression reminiscent of that during the Cultural Revolution. Present-day China is widely seen as a threat to democratic societies and it faces collective containment, led by the United States, from the Western countries. It has become a formidable force that concerns both Hong Kong and Taiwan.

However, China could have turned out to be different from what it is today. There was a time when China could have taken a different path. If, thirty-plus years ago, during the massive pro-democracy movement in China, the authorities had refrained from repression, today's China might not only have avoided becoming the world's biggest troublemaker but it might even have become a member of the community of democratic societies.

If the Chinese Communist Party (CCP) had not taken repressive actions, the reformist forces represented by Zhao Ziyang undoubtedly could have been consolidated. Zhao Ziyang was the senior CCP leader most inclined toward market-oriented economic reforms and he had a relatively more open-minded approach. If Zhao Ziyang had been given further decision-making power, he likely would have guided China in the direction of deeper market-oriented reforms. This possible trend can be glimpsed from the promotion of the "Bankruptcy Law" that began in 1988. In other words, if the events of 1989 had succeeded, China would not have experienced chaos but instead it would have embarked on a more resolute pace of economic reform.

If the CCP had not taken repressive action, the political reforms that began in 1988 might have advanced naturally with strong public support, particularly for press freedoms. This means that the economic reforms would have been conducted in an environment with robust media supervision. Even today, the CCP acknowledges that only by strengthening media supervision can it effectively contain the widespread corruption in the country. Thus, if freedom of speech had been expanded as early as 1989, corruption would be plaguing the Chinese system as it is today.

If, back in the day, the CCP had not taken repressive actions and had instead set a precedent for state-society dialogue, the fact is that the 1987 political report of the 13th National Congress of the CCP, under the leadership of Bao Tong, had already established the direction of focusing on social negotiation and dialogue as a key aspect of reform. The students' call for dialogue was, in fact, in line with this advocacy for reform of the political system. In today's China, the image of the government and the people working together with one heart and one mind is long gone, and people's trust in the government is non-existent. This lack of trust is a major reason why so many social conflicts ultimately escalate. As reform enters a new stage where there is a power struggle between state and society, the fundamental guarantee for social stability is a state-society channel for dialogue Only through such dialogue can both parties work together to ensure a smooth transition. Taiwan's experience serves as the best reference in this regard. Therefore, if the 1989 pro-democracy movement had succeeded, it can be imagined that the social environment for reform today would have been much more stable.

Of course, if the CCP had not resorted to repression, the reforms would have had a much more profound impact on China's political, economic, and social development, but it would have taken time for that impact to be revealed.

At the very least, however, the above three points are trends we can predict seeing in the short term. Simply put, if the CCP had not resorted to repression, China would have more quickly entered the track of market-oriented economic development, and that economic development would have occurred within a framework of political democracy, thus reducing the impact of the serious issues of social injustice that we are seeing today. Such social development would have taken place through continuous state-social dialogue, and it would have contributed to the growth of a civil society. Such a China undoubtedly would have been welcomed by the entire world.

However, the CCP did open fire and suppress the student movement. This repression caused China to lose its most precious opportunity in the past one hundred years for dialogue between the government and the public, which could have jointly promoted China's smooth transition toward constitutional democracy and a market economy. Such a golden opportunity was lost to the sound of gunfire, and perhaps it never again will reappear.

About China's Pro-Democracy Movement

Question 35: Is putting "human rights first" treating the symptom rather than the root cause?

On April 20th, U.S. Secretary of State Blinken held a video conference with human rights advocates representing eight countries to discuss America's human rights policy. Chinese human rights lawyer, Teng Biao, advised Secretary Blinken that priority should be placed on human rights in the U.S. government's foreign policy.

By adopting this approach, the U.S. State Department would be signaling to the worldwide authoritarian nations that it prioritizes human rights in its diplomatic policies, a stance that has been consistent since President Carter, that is, emphasizing American values through human rights issues. While I used to support the idea of putting "human rights first" in foreign policy, my perspective has shifted due to changing circumstances. I cannot agree with Lawyer Teng Biao's proposal of placing human rights at the forefront of U.S. diplomacy.

Of course, the issue of human rights is a crucial concern, and it is commendable that as a global leader, the United States should raise human rights issues. However, employing a "human rights first" foreign policy in dealing with China is misguided and will be ineffective. Resolving human rights issues with China will require first addressing the political problems. Without addressing China's political issues, human rights problems will remain unsolved and such a stance will only result in empty slogans. In China, even economic issues are intertwined with political matters, let alone human rights. Hence, when formulating its foreign policy toward China, the U.S. State Department should prioritize political issues, with human rights resolutions falling under political problem-solving.

For years, the United States has consistently emphasized "human rights first," but the actual impact has been limited. For instance, in the case of China, the greatest success of human rights diplomacy has been the release of a few political prisoners, myself included. I am grateful for the efforts made by the Western countries in promoting human rights. However, the resolution of individual cases does not lead to an overall improvement in China's human rights situation. In fact, after Wei Jingsheng, Wang Juntao, and I, as prominent political prisoners, were released, China's human rights situation deteriorated even further. The Chinese Communist Party (CCP) quickly arrested Liu Xiaobo who eventually died in prison. History has proven that human rights diplomacy cannot fundamentally solve human rights issues. This is a painful lesson.

Furthermore, in response to Western countries' human rights diplomatic efforts, the CCP has learned to use Chinese citizens as hostages, arresting dissidents who can be used as leverage during periods of tensions in Sino-U.S. relations. Consequently, a "human rights first" policy paradoxically may lead to Chinese dissidents being used as bargaining chips.

To be clear, I am not saying that a "human rights first" policy is wrong, nor am I suggesting that the U.S. should abandon pressuring China on human rights issues. My point is that although human rights should be a focal point in U.S. policy toward China, the most critical aspect of U.S. policy should be addressing China's political issues. This should include two elements: first, cooperating with allies to collectively deter the external expansion of the CCP; second, joining forces with pro-democracy movements both inside and outside of China, utilizing various means – political, economic, military – to destabilize CCP rule. Only by ending the CCP's one-party dictatorship can there be a chance of improving China's human rights situation.

During, the past twenty years, from our perspective as Chinese dissidents seeking refuge in Western countries, we have gained new insights and developed new strategies regarding China and the CCP. If the most crucial aspect of foreign policy and our core thinking continues to be solely focused on "human rights" issues, we will fall into the trap set by the CCP.

Question 36: What are Wang Juntao's political views?

Recently, the think-tank "Dialogue China" organized an event for renowned overseas activist Wang Juntao to launch his new book, Action and Transformation: Reflections on China's Democratization. Having been deeply involved in China's pro-democracy movement for years, in this book Wang Juntao presents a series of thought-provoking views. Here, I will provide a brief overview of some of his ideas to offer insight to those concerned about China's democratization.

In this new book, Wang Juntao emphasizes that as the world's second-largest economic power, China's democratization is crucial for global peace and security. Transforming China into a peaceful and democratic nation is an essential task to ensure world peace and freedom in the 21st century. This point is of paramount importance as there is a misconception prevailing in Taiwan, Hong Kong, the United States, and other Western countries that suggests that democratization is solely an internal Chinese affair and other nations have no obligation to support it. This view overlooks a significant reality, as Wang Juntao asserts in his book, China's challenges are not confined to China alone – they are global issues.

When analyzing China's current political situation and the potential paths for its future transformation, Wang Juntao disagrees with the common expectation that there can be a peaceful transition in China. Instead, he believes that the possibility of a social revolution is quite likely. His judgment is based on the concept of "violence dependence," whereby, as he points out, the Chinese Communist Party (CCP) has grown accustomed to and has become reliant on ruling through violence. On the one hand, the government sees immediate results from the use of violence, leading to a decreasing willingness to govern through reason and dialogue. On the other hand, the consequences of violence breed opposition between state and society, eventually leading to a tendency for civil society to resort to violence in response. Wang contends that, in a situation where both sides believe in the efficacy of violence, the hope for a peaceful transition becomes increasingly elusive. Although this is not a desirable scenario, I must acknowledge that in contemporary China, slogans promoting "peaceful, rational, and non-violent" means are increasingly being questioned, and instances of the glorification of violent resistance, as in the case of Yang Jia, validate Wang Juntao's assessment.

In the context of the prerequisites for a democratic transition Wang Juntao specifically reminds us that based on historical experience, in the past most societies' democratic transitions did not occur when democratic ideals had deeply penetrated the people's hearts. Instead, these transitions were primarily driven by interests. Based on this, Wang Juntao offers guiding advice for China's overseas democracy activists and opposition movements: they must regard democracy as the best solution aligning with their interests. In my understanding, constructive opposition forces must present demands that align with the people's interests, such as a more equitable distribution of social resources, rather than merely focusing on the promotion of ideology and the mobilization of the masses.

Finally, addressing the various outside criticisms directed at the overseas democracy movements, Wang Juntao puts forth a rather profound perspective. He believes that democracy movements aim to establish a political system that involves the participation of the entire population, and a country's democratization is a central concern of the entire collective citizenry. In the political struggle preceding a transition, democracy movements primarily disseminate democratic ideas and work to promote a transition. They cannot be held responsible for nations or populations that, as a whole, do not embrace democratic ideals. Those who have not actively participated in a democratic movement do not have a moral right to criticize the performance of the democracy movement. Democracy movements often engage in self-reflection and self-criticism, and they blame themselves based on external criticism due to a lack of clarity about their role. It seems as if they believe that they can singlehandedly bring about a country's transition to democracy. This misalignment occurs when they exaggerate their role and assume that establishing a democratic system is solely their responsibility. This perspective may be subject to different interpretations, but it is worthwhile for those outside the movement to take it into consideration..

Amid the uncertainty in China's political landscape, we need more thoughtful deliberations on the prospects for a future transformation. I recommend reading Wang Juntao's new book to inspire further discussions on this subject.

Question 37: Why did we feel the need to establish the "Dialogue China" think- tank?

After Xi Jinping came to power in 2012, China underwent astonishing changes. Internally, Chinese Communist Party (CCP) rule shifted from authoritarianism to totalitarianism, while externally, China expanded its global political, economic, and ideological influence. Some describe this era as dark, but history often shows that after dark times, dawn will emerge. Therefore, what is occurring in China today does not mean that democracy is no longer possible there. On the contrary, the immense uncertainty might offer us opportunities we have never considered. The establishment of "Dialogue China" is our collective effort to prepare for such opportunities.

"Dialogue China" aims to bring together individuals, whether Chinese or non-Chinese, who aspire to see change occur in China. We seek to foster dialogue among different political forces and reach a consensus on China's future challenges, including issues concerning Taiwan, Tibet, Xinjiang, and Hong Kong. "Dialogue China" will not dwell simply on slogans by the opposition but it will strive to propose concrete policies, systems, and plans. We will analyze the current realities in China, but our primary focus is on ensuring a smooth and peaceful transition toward constitutional democracy after the transformation.

The members of the "Dialogue China" group include intellectuals and students who attempted to promote democracy in China in 1989. For more than three decades, we have not forgotten nor have we given up on our mission. We envision "Dialogue China" to be another attempt and a fresh start 30-plus years later. Additionally, we recognize that China's future transformation requires new forces. Thus, our team also comprises representatives from the post-1990s generation, the new middle class, and overseas Chinese. We understand that the impact of China's change on neighboring regions cannot be ignored, which is why we have young political representatives from Taiwan and Hong Kong on our team. This diverse group will present a professional and youthful face, highlighting the collective strength of a Chinese global civil society after 30-plus years of experience and lessons.

We are well aware that we will face numerous challenges, but we are confident about the future because we stand on the right side of history. We know that the changes we anticipate will not come quickly, nor will they come easily, but we are determined to reach our goals step by step, with patience and perseverance. Our objective is crystal clear: we look forward to the establishment of a future China that is free, just, prosperous, and civilized, and that allows the Chinese people to regain respect on the world stage.

Question 38: Do Chinese people not want democracy?

I once attended a book club organized by the University of Maryland's Taiwanese Students Association, where, as requested by the host, I shared some of my views on China-related issues. During the Q&A session, an American student asked me about a prevailing belief that many Chinese people care more about their immediate personal interests; as long as they can make money and have their basic needs met, they are not interested in democracy. He wanted to know my perspective on this issue.

I understand that this is a common confusion among many Westerners because they do not see a strong interest in democracy when interacting with Chinese. However, if Chinese people truly have no interest in democracy, then how can we explain the political fervor during the Cultural Revolution, even though it was highly distorted? How can we explain the nationwide democratic movement in 1989? How can we explain the recent protests in front of the government building in Changsha, where retired soldiers chanted slogans demanding the mayor's resignation? Are these people not Chinese?

To understand this issue, I recommend a book by Ian Johnson called Wild Grass: Three Portraits of Change in Modern China (Eight Flags Culture, 2016). Ian Johnson, whose Chinese name is Zhang Yan, is a sinology master's graduate from the Free University of Berlin. He reported on China as Beijing correspondent for The Wall Street Journal and later for the New

York Time. In 2001 he won the Pulitzer Prize for his series on the persecution of the Falun Gong movement. His direct observations of grassroots people and their collective psychology provide valuable insights for understanding the pulse of Chinese society.

In this book, there is a passage that helps to answer the American student's question. Johnson writes, "We often read that Chinese people don't care about politics, aren't interested in democracy, and are content to worry only about themselves. Chinese often say the same thing about themselves. But by 'politics,' most people mean that they do not want to be caught up in government campaigns or power struggles within the Communist Party – that is, what most people consider 'politics.' Ask them if they care about corruption or about officials abusing their power, and you suddenly get a different answer: they care a lot" (p.158).

This commentary highlights the crux of the issue: when we say that Chinese people do not care about democracy, we should first define what we mean by "democracy." If we discuss democracy from an elite perspective, where it involves complex political choices such as presidential or parliamentary systems, or if we see it as a political ethic of protecting the rights of minorities while obeying the will of the majority, then indeed most Chinese people may not show significant interest. After all, in a China where even the most basic forms of democracy, such as elections and freedom of speech, do not yet exist, such discussions might seem somewhat luxurious. However, as observed by Johnson, when we view democracy from the grassroots level, understanding it as people wanting corrupt officials to be punished and feeling aggrieved when the people's rights are violated, we can see that enthusiasm for democracy among Chinese people is actually quite high.

The misconception that "Chinese people don't care about democracy" arises because, at the current stage of China's development, interest in democracy is closely tied to immediate self-interest, and it has not yet evolved into a pursuit of universal, ideational democracy. In contrast, Western democratic countries, interest in such universal ideational democracy is already prevalent. In other words, when Westerners evaluate China based on their own understanding of democracy, they might perceive a lack of interest among Chinese people. However, if they adjust their definition of democracy to a basic level, they will discover that Chinese people are indeed very enthusiastic about democracy.

Question 39: How does the Chinese Communist Party suppress opposition forces?

It is well known that the Chinese Communist Party (CCP) is an autocratic and corrupt ruling party that opposes any democratic movements. Despite this, the CCP has been able to maintain stable governance without encountering much strong opposition. But this phenomenon cannot simply be explained by the notion that "Chinese people are afraid to resist," because throughout its long history, China experienced numerous changes in its ruling dynasties, suggesting a willingness to challenge authority.

Certainly, the prevalence of cynicism has weakened the moral appeal of opposition forces. However, opposition forces have always existed within China, and whenever an opportunity arises, the opposition will attempt to voice an appeal. The "Charter 08" movement is an example such an underground movement that emerged for a brief period. But why is it that opposition forces in China are unable to constitute a significant challenge to CCP rule?

While there certainly are problems within the opposition forces themselves, it is not the focus here and will be discussed separately. What must be acknowledged here is that the CCP has been effective strategically and tactically in suppressing the opposition forces, thereby successfully inhibiting their growth. Unless this impasse is broken, the opposition forces in China will not be able develop. Overall, such suppression takes place in five main respects:

• The first respect is the blatant use of violence. It can be assumed that events like June 4th (the Tiananmen Square protests) are a thing of the past, and the CCP will no longer rely on violent means to rule. However, the powerful stability maintenance apparatus of the CCP, including the military, armed police, state security, and public security, remains the fundamental pillar enabling stable state governance. The CCP may not always resort to direct force, but the threat of force looms every day, always ready to deal with the opposition. Remember why writer Yu Jie was forced to flee to the United States? After being kidnapped by the police, his five fingers were nearly broken, and he was severely beaten, leaving him no choice but to leave the country. In this regard, the CCP does not need support from the underworld; the CCP itself is the underworld.

• The second respect is economic means. Over the years, the CCP has maintained stability through significant economic growth, which brings enormous national resources. The CCP employs these resources in three ways: (1) to buy off a group of elites, turning them into a new interest group and incorporating them into the current system, thus ensuring that they do not join opposition forces; (2) to use stability maintenance funds to pacify mass incidents, ensuring they do not become the basis for opposition forces; and (3) to employ economic development as a dazzling display, capturing people's attention and diverting their focus from public affairs. All three measures have basically achieved their purposes.

•   The third respect is a preemptive strike tactic. The CCP learned from the lessons of the 1989 Chinese democratic movement and the collapse of authoritarianism in Eastern Europe, and early on it decided on adopting the tactic of "eliminating all opposition forces in their infancy," also known as a "preemptive strike." Whenever the CCP suspects that certain individuals or forces might form an opposition, it immediately launches a severe crackdown. In such an environment of preemptive strikes, it naturally is very difficult for any opposition forces to grow. This is why I consistently oppose the argument that "Chinese people lack the courage to resist, Chinese people are weak": it is easy to talk without experiencing the harsh reality. Why don't you try living in such a ruthless environment?

•   The fourth respect is propaganda. Although the traditional mainstream ideology has completely collapsed and when the authorities speak, the people laugh in ridicule, the CCP has learned not to directly tell lies. Rather, it uses statements that sound plausible and sincere on the surface. However, upon careful analysis, it becomes apparent that they are merely linguistic traps. The problem is that most Chinese people are unwilling to analyze things carefully, which allows CCP propaganda to effectively smear and refute the opposition forces, and even to divide.

•   Finally, the fifth respect is social control. With economic development, social stratification has become increasingly serious in China, and indeed, state control over society has decreased to some extent. However, I must say that the decrease in state control is somewhat limited. From real-name registration required for internet use to censorship of sensitive words, from blacklists for returnees to ID management, from unit surveillance to state security interrogations, the ability of the CCP to assert social control is not as relaxed as external observers might think. It remains a country and a society under highly controlled conditions. In such an environment, the growth of any opposition forces is undeniably challenging.

In summary, the lack of a strong opposition force in China is largely due to the CCP's effective and continuously evolving methods of suppression.

Question 40: Why is the Chinese Communist Party so afraid of the June 4th "turmoil"?

Every year, on the anniversary of the June 4th incident, the authorities in Beijing respond as if they are facing a major threat and they employ the most severe surveillance measures since 1989. Why is it that over 30 years later, the Chinese Communist Party (CCP) remains so anxious, even increasingly so, about June 4th? The nervousness behind this reaction reveals several issues.

The first issue is that the CCP authorities themselves inadvertently are proving the fact that the Chinese people have not forgotten about June 4th. For a long time, it seemed as if the outside world believed that under the tight blockade imposed by the CCP, Chinese people had already forgotten about June 4th, especially the members of the younger generations who seemed to be unaware of it. If that were indeed the case, then why would the Beijing authorities be so anxious? The CCP clearly knows something that those outside China do not: June 4th remains the most sensitive nerve in Chinese society. People may not openly talk about it, or they may even lie and claim to have forgotten, but in reality, no one has forgotten, and the members of the younger generations are even more curious about it. The authorities' nervousness is justified.

The second issue is that the Xi Jinping regime lacks confidence in itself. In general, those who are very anxious and fearful internally, and those who lack self-assurance often display an inexplicable nervousness. The intensity of the stability maintenance efforts that are seen in China are seldom seen elsewhere, leaving virtually no room for dissent within the country. Nevertheless, despite such measures, the CCP is still extremely nervous, and with even the slightest movement or whisper by the opposition, it acts as if it is facing a major enemy. This demonstrates that the authorities are not as invincible as some might imagine, and their rule is not as stable as they would like others to believe. Such nervousness is simply an admission of their vulnerability. A person without confidence typically avoids conflict. For Xi Jinping, it is best to suppress the issue of June 4th with maximum force because he has no idea how to deal with it. Therefore, any expectation that Xi Jinping will proactively resolve the June 4th issue during his tenure is simply overestimating him.

The third issue is that the June 4th incident remains an important political variable. Significant historical legacies are crucial factors in driving contemporary social transformations. As long as these issues remain unresolved, they will not lose their historical potency. Today, June 4th has become a symbol in China, representing a wide range of political forces: resistance, democracy, collective resentment, anti-corruption, historical memory, transitional justice, the future, hope, and more. These political forces must grasp a legitimate banner to highlight their strength, and it is here where June 4th serves as the most significant foundation for legitimacy. Once this issue is triggered, a comprehensive transformation will become unstoppable, which is why the authorities are doing everything in their power to prevent the Pandora's box of June 4th from being opened.

The fourth issue is that CCP rule undoubtedly faces significant pressure. I recently participated in numerous commemorations of June 4th, which left me physically exhausted and forced me to see a doctor due to excessive stress. The doctor diagnosed me with nerve fatigue and psychological tension and he advised me to take a proper rest. In this regard, the CCP and I can be said to share the same illness. The CCP is clearly under immense pressure, which leads to its jittery behavior, as if it is shooting at shadows. An intriguing question thus arises: First, what exactly is causing such enormous pressures for the CCP? Second, what exactly are these great pressures that they cause the CCP to experience such psychological fatigue? Third, although I could take a proper rest after June 4th, the CCP cannot possibly rest like I can (although I wish it would). So, how much longer can the CCP, carrying such immense pressures, hold on?

Question 41: Why haven't the members of China's middle class become advocates for democracy?

According to social development theory, the rise of a middle class should lead to demands for democratization. This prediction is not only a common expectation in the West about China's future but also a self-comforting thought among many within China who are reluctant to face political change. However, this view is not universally applicable and has both correct and incorrect aspects when applied to China's unique context.

It is incorrect because, unlike the Western concept of a civics class that is politically independent from the state, China's so-called middle class is not entirely separate from the political power and state apparatus. Instead, to a large extent the Chinese middle class is part of the state's power structure, or at least, the members of the Chinese middle class are closely associated to the power structure. The relationship between the middle class and the government can be described as mutually dependent – they prosper and suffer together.

There are two noteworthy news stories about wealthy individuals. One is from China: Wang Yuanshan, chairman of Wang Pangzi Construction Company in Xiangfan, Hubei province, with assets worth billions of yuan, once stated, "In my lifetime, I will donate all my wealth of over a billion yuan to the government." The other news story comes from a foreign country: On January 25, 2008, Bill Gates announced at the

World Economic Forum in Switzerland that he would donate three billion US dollars to improve the lives of people in Africa, providing seeds, fertilizers, and agricultural techniques to enhance the crop yields for African farmers.

Living abroad, it is not surprising to hear about wealthy people donating their assets, as it is quite common in countries like the United States. Many civil society foundations, educational institutions, and cultural facilities in the U.S. have been established based on substantial donations. Giving back to society has become a social mechanism. We hope this mechanism will someday take root in China as well, and we expect the rise of a new wealthy class in China will develop a habit of giving back to society. However, today we see wealthy individuals in China beginning to show an awareness of making donations, but the recipients are not the tens of millions of their compatriots living below the poverty line; instead, they are donating to the government with the world's highest foreign exchange reserves. We often talk about China's unique situation, and this might just be one such example. The attitude of donating to the government may sound somewhat absurd, but it reflects a deep-seated issue in the midst of China's societal transformation, which is the problem of social relations within the middle class.

You can think about why Jack Ma, co-founder of the Alibaba Group, publicly expressed support for Deng Xiaoping's decision to use force in 1989, or why Xi Jinping's sister once held substantial shares in the company of China's richest man, Wang Jianlin. Also, you can look at the relationship between former Minister of Railways Liu Zhijun and wealthy Shanxi businessperson Ding Shumiao. From these examples, you can see that the so-called "middle class" in China does not exist in opposition to the government but rather it is interdependent with the government.

Thus, expecting this kind of middle class to support social and political reforms that aim to decentralize state power is like trying to take a tiger's skin. In fact, political reforms not only threaten the interests of those in power but they also affect those in the middle class. Therefore, not only will the middle classes not become advocates for democratization but they may also become forces hindering it.

However, it is correct to say that for the theory of the rise of a middle class leading to democratization to become a reality in China, there must first exist a genuine middle class. This middle class should no longer rely on its relationship with the state to accumulate wealth, and it should be fully independent from the state. Such a middle classes should be rooted in society rather than the state and its interests should be aligned with those of society. Only this kind of middle class can make demands for social change; its donations will flow toward civil society rather than to government institutions or merely to charity work. When independent non-governmental organizations, outspoken media outlets, and even political opposition movements begin to receive economic support from this kind of middle class, the democratization of China will truly begin. This is why we are hopeful about China's future. We therefore should have high expectations for such an emerging, genuine middle class that bears the historical mission of advancing democratization. and we should have high expectations for them.

Question 42: Will globalization necessarily benefit China's democratization?

During the New Year's holiday in 2015, while vacationing in Japan, I had the opportunity to meet and chat with some locals, including two young Chinese students studying abroad. I was surprised by their level of awareness about universal values, their understanding of democratic ideals, their criticism of the state in China today, and their unwavering confidence in the future. In our conversations, their calm demeanor and composure were far different from the stereotypical image of the self-focused consumerism that is commonly associated with Chinese youth, leading me to exclaim, "Heroes have always emerged from the younger generation."

When I inquired about their future plans, they both expressed their intention to pursue their educations and to seek job opportunities in the United States due to the economic downturn in Japan, making it challenging for them to find work there after graduation. They implied that they had no plans to return to China to work unless fundamental changes were to occur there. Upon hearing this, my exclamation turned into a sigh of disappointment.

Over the years, the impact of globalization on China and the country's more open attitude toward talent outflows have resulted in a noticeable trend of elite young Chinese choosing to emigrate. Many top students from prestigious universities in China early on aspire to study abroad, and this trend seems to be on the rise. In theory, their studying abroad, and thereby being influenced by Western democratic societies, should have a positive impact on China's future democratization. This was also observed in the early 20th century when Chinese students who studied in Japan, Europe, and the United States returned home and became the mainstay of liberal intellectuals driving social change from the May Fourth Movement to the late 1940s. These returned students actively participated in social reforms and promoted the growth of civil society. This process continued until the Communist regime, with its establishment in 1949, forcibly ended it. However, expectations for the current generation of Chinese students abroad may not necessarily replicate the same outcomes, as a sizable portion of those abroad are choosing to remain overseas rather than returning to China. In other words, they have voted with their feet, making the choice to "exit" and to step away from efforts to drive change within China. This is, in fact, a negative factor for China's future democratization.

Of course, I have no intention of criticizing the choices of this generation, as everyone has the right to prioritize their personal interests. However, objectively speaking, the emergence of this new wave of emigration benefits the maintenance of China's existing system and is unfavorable to societal transformation. Economist Albert O. Hirschman in his book Exit, Voice, and Loyalty concludes that if there is an opportunity to exit, those who are most dissatisfied with the system and have the potential to effect change are also the ones most likely to choose emigration. This will significantly weaken domestic calls for change and delay the process of democratization. Hirschman further points out that some authoritarian regimes are aware of this and utilize it to consolidate power. Looking back at China's reforms and opening since the 1990s and the policy of the regime to send dissidents into exile, we can see faint traces of such a development in China. In other words, while openness to the outside world is beneficial to democratization, in other respects it can also be detrimental to democratization. Thus, we should not make sweeping generalizations and we must acknowledge the complexity of this issue.

The Chinese students in Japan whom I mentioned earlier, I believe, would make significant contributions to China if they were to return to China and participate in societal reforms. I am convinced that many of the talented youths from their generation possess similar qualities. However, a significant portion of them will choose to exit. This choice is fortunate for them as they can avoid dealing with the existing system and living in the difficult Chinese environment. They may be happy to leave China, but the Communist Party is also pleased. This is the reason for my sigh of disappointment.

Question 43: Why can it be said that anti-communism is a form of civilization-building?

I have never shied away from admitting that my political stance is anti-Communist. In this day and age, being "anti-Communist" may seem old-fashioned. Many old-timers who used to be anti-Communist have now abandoned that position. So why do I still choose this old-fashioned political stance?

What relieves me is that no one can accuse me of being anti-Communist for personal gain or ambition. Nowadays, no matter where you are, it seems easier to advance in your career or achieve prosperity by flattering the Communist Party, or at least by not opposing it. Those who are anti-Communist are seen as outsiders and are looked down upon by those seeking personal gain. It is definitely not a convenient or advantageous position to hold.

Therefore, the question remains: why do I persist in being anti-Communist? The reason is actually quite simple: I cannot overlook certain aspects of communism. I believe that political positions can differ, and we should respect each other's political views. However, the difference between me and the Chinese Communist Party (CCP) is not primarily a difference about political ideology at this moment. What I find unacceptable is the Communist Party's actions, which consistently lower the standards of human civilization. When it comes to civilization, there is no room for us to step back.

Let me provide two examples from my personal experience to illustrate my point about civilization.

The first example is related to language. Those familiar with internet slang know that it is quite simple to identify comments by the "50 cent party" – they indiscriminately use foul language, resort to personal attacks, and engage in baseless arguments. One might argue that some individuals not associated with the "50 cent party" may also engage in such offensive behavior, but what distinguishes them from the "50 cent party"? Engaging in "50 cent party" behavior without receiving money is just as bad as being an official member. Each one of us, including those who are part of the "50 Cent party," has learned basic norms of civility during our upbringing, such as not insulting or physically harming others. These are principles taught as early as kindergarten, part of basic civics education. However, the Communist Party–trained internet workers resort primarily to malicious and harmful language. This is not merely a political difference; it is a matter of civilization. If we allow this Communist Party–style to spread, we will be failing to uphold the basic civilized standard of "not insulting others."

The second example is related to behavior. Not long ago, the official Chinese media published an article accusing me of "colluding" with the "Church of Almighty God" in China and ordering support for violent terrorist activities within the country. Another official media outlet even published a comment labeling the democracy movement I was part of as a "cult." In reality, I do not know anyone from the "Church of Almighty God," let alone issuing orders to support them. The letter exposing me, signed by "Wang Youcai," and circulating on the internet was entirely fabricated. If this were just something said by someone online, I would not pay any attention to it, as we all know that many people fabricate things they put on the internet. However, when an official media outlet from a major country fabricates stories without any basis, it completely crosses the boundaries of civilization. This demonstrates that the Chinese government is willing to disregard the basic norms of civilization to suppress an individual. If the Communist Party's actions succeed and it continues to be welcomed and praised, can we still claim to be a civilized society?

Yes, the Communist Party is powerful, and it has driven prosperity and economic growth. But at the same time, some of the actions by this regime go against the norms of civilization that humanity has painstakingly built up over hundreds of years. More critically, the Communist Party relies on its power to force many countries, politicians, and individuals to turn a blind eye to CCP actions, making them accomplices in destroying the foundations of civilization. This kind of Communist Party is using violence to drag human society down with it to beneath the surface of civilization. For anyone who has even the slightest hope for a civilized and free society, what reason can there be for not opposing communism?

About Taiwan, Hong Kong, Xinjiang, and Tibet

Question 44: Do All Chinese Support the Reunification of Taiwan with the mainland?

Along with the rapid spread of the Wuhan coronavirus epidemic, Taiwan public opinion and emotions began to turn against mainland China. Confronted by the long-term political repression inflicted by the Chinese Communist Party (CCP) and the sharp increase in nativist consciousness brought about by Taiwan's internal political and social developments, the emergence of nationalist sentiments on Taiwan is completely understandable and largely irreproachable. However, I believe that a mature society – even if it has a herd mentality – should be founded on facts, not emotions.

What worries me the most is the herd mentality of some Chinese netizens that is pervasive on the internet. These netizens assume all Chinese people, including the democracy activists, support reunification. They assume all Chinese support reunification. Even if China democratizes – they believe – the democracy activists will still want to reclaim Taiwan. That is not true.

Let me give you a small example: I recently attended a

small-scale Sino-U.S. relations salon in Washington D.C. The speaker was Brig. Gen. Robert S. Spalding III, author of the book Stealth War, who assumed the position of Special Assistant to the U.S. Air Force Vice Chief of Staff in February 2018 and former U.S. Defense Attaché, US Embassy, Beijing. At a one point in the discussion, a girl from Taiwan raised her hand and asked a casual question: If China changes the status quo across the Taiwan Strait, how will the United States respond? General Spalding answered in a straightforward military style, saying, "We would choose to stand with Taiwan." But that is not the reason I am mentioning this.

The main point is that before the general had even finished speaking, the entire whole audience exploded in applause. This was the most enthusiastic applause of the entire event, expressing the high level of agreement and appreciation of the audience for General Spalding's response. Among those applauding, 90 percent were from mainland China (I believe the girl from Taiwan who asked the question can attest to that). In other words, at least 90 percent of the participants at the event were in support of U.S. protection of Taiwan, not support of unification by force. This was not surprising to me because I was familiar with almost half of those in the audience. I know that their position on the Taiwan issue is the same as mine. We all oppose CCP reunification of Taiwan by force, and we all believe that the Taiwanese people themselves should determine the future of the island.

Okay, one can say I am a moderate. But at least one cannot

deny that moderates exist. One cannot claim that all Chinese are fanatical ultra-nationalists who are prepared to go to war to reclaim Taiwan. One should know that there are many Chinese people who sympathize with Taiwan and who are willing to stand with Taiwan against CCP intimidation. I am willing to stand with Taiwan. Of course, one can say that these are the views of a minority of Chinese people. Most Chinese are brainwashed by reunification propaganda. I totally agree, I admit that clear-thinking Chinese are indeed a minority. However, this minority is still made up of people. You cannot ignore their existence because they are few in number. When one cannot discern between right and wrong, is indiscriminate in judgment, and disregards this minority when Chinese people post incendiary comments on reunification, one's analysis is flawed.

I have repeatedly stated that I understand the antipathy Taiwan and Hong Kong people feel toward mainland China. Those who familiar with me know that in the confrontation of public opinion across the Taiwan Strait, I am on the side of Taiwan and Hong Kong. However, I must emphasize: One's moral high ground should be founded on facts, not emotions.

From my understanding of the CCP, its large-scale propaganda work must also include planting fake Taiwanese and Hong Kong commentators who post radical statements on the internet, stimulating emotional confrontations among the people on the three sides of the Strait [mainland-Taiwan–Hong Kong]. Conflict among these people, and hostile feelings based on ethnic identity, are precisely the things that authoritarian governments prefer to see. Given the pressure and challenges the CCP was facing due to the pandemic, the most likely way to calm the anger of the Chinese people at this moment was to divert their attention away from China's poor management of the epidemic. And what better way was there to do that than to stir up nationalist emotions? At that time, when emotions were running high and basic distinctions were overlooked in directly judging others, such a surge in public sentiment plays right into the CCP's trap. Apart from venting emotions, it brings no benefit to Taiwan's interests

Question 45: What Are the reasons for the Chinese Communist Party's frequent provocations against Taiwan?

For some time now, the Chinese Communist Party (CCP) has taken a series of actions that are interpreted by the international community as targeting Taiwan. Let us analyze them. First, Xi Jinping – as chairman of the Central Military Commission of the CCP – in June 2022 signed the Draft Law Regulating the Chinese People's Liberation Army's "Military Operations Other than War," which is thought to be preparation for imitating Russia's invasion of Ukraine under the euphemism of a "special military operation." Second, China's Foreign Ministry declared that the Taiwan Strait consisted of China's internal waters. The implication of this action is the beginning of a unilateral declaration of sovereignty over Taiwan. Although it is clear that the United States and other Western nations will not acknowledge this declaration, it is possible that such a position is preparation for a future war in the Taiwan Strait. The third action is that when China's Defense Minister Wei Fenghe gave a speech at the Shangri-La Conference in Singapore on June 12, 2022, he took a hardline position and said that, if necessary, "the People's Liberation Army is prepared to go to war, and fight until the finish." This was the first time the phrase "fight until the finish" had appeared, and it can be seen as an escalation of the rhetoric of military threats against Taiwan. The fourth action was to announce the launch of China's third aircraft carrier, the Type 003 aircraft carrier "Fujian." This is considered a milestone in the development of armaments and a declaration of China's military strength to the United States. The fifth action was that 29 Chinese military aircraft violated Taiwan's air space on June 21, 2022, the third most aircraft in 2022.

This combination of actions, and the fact that they all took place within a month may not necessarily mean that the leadership in Beijing has definitively concluded it is incapable of launching an attack on Taiwan. However, the intent to challenge the United States regarding the Taiwan issue and demonstrate against Taiwan's democratically elected government has become very apparent. So, how should we view this series of actions by the CCP? Has Xi Jinping really made a decision to initiate a war? In general, I think all these external actions are a function of internal factors within the CCP.

First, we should not absolutely rule out the possibility that Xi Jinping may order the use of military force against Taiwan. Many people say that the CCP would definitely lose if it were to use military force against Taiwan and therefore it will never dare to attack Taiwan. Such a misjudgment is the result of not learning from historical experience. How many people really believed that the CCP would use the People's Liberation Army to carry out such a violent military operation during the Beijing massacre in 1989? That the CCP will disregard all bounds of human civilization for its own political interests should be considered normal. One should not judge the Communist Party's thinking by the standards of the civilized world. This was especially true before the opening of the critical 20th National Congress of the

CCP in October 2022. There were rumors both inside and outside of China that Xi Jinping's authority was being challenged inside the CCP due to his political line of allying with Russia against the United States and his inflexible "zero-Covid" pandemic prevention policy, which led to a near collapse of the economy. If such information were true, it would be logical for Xi Jinping to create tensions on the Taiwan issue, launch a new patriotic fever, and seize the opportunity to consolidate his authority in order to bring about a smooth re-election to an unprecedented third term as paramount leader. For Xi Jinping, this could be a perfect way to use the conflict to fulfill his personal ambitions. In this regard, the international community should not project its wishful thinking onto Xi Jinping's recklessness.

Second, those who know the history of the CCP's policy toward Taiwan should know that the threat of military force has always been an important element in its bluff and bluster. Even when Taiwan's President Lee Teng-hui visited the United States in 1996, the Chinese side launched missiles (which later proved to be unarmed) into Taiwan's coastal waters,. The Taiwan issue has always been a card used by the CCP to deal with domestic issues. When domestic problems arise in China, the creation of conflict over the Taiwan Strait has often been the best option for the CCP to divert the attention of the domestic public. After Shanghai's pandemic prevention measures triggered popular indignation, social conflicts in China began to rise. The Xuzhou chained woman incident and the Tangshan restaurant attack attracted billions of hits online, a reflection that the collective social mood was already unstable. Under such circumstances, a series of actions to heat up the atmosphere on the Taiwan issue may be the CCP's smug calculation. There is, of course, another possibility: the CCP does not yet really want to use force against Taiwan. The purpose of its series of bluffing is actually to target the Chinese people and to try to divert their attention away from domestic problems.

In short, we should not lessen our vigilance against a Communist Party invasion of Taiwan, but we should also recognize that the threats against Taiwan may also be targeted at the development of social conflicts within China.

Question 46: Why have the people of Hong Kong reached a breaking point?

After the Umbrella Revolution erupted in Hong Kong, whenever the authorities attempted to forcefully disperse the protesters, more than a 100,000 people would come out at night to show their support. With such backing, the authorities had limited options. This is a crucial reason why the movement could continue for so long. Why did the people of Hong Kong stand firm? When looking at the historical context, there are at least nine reasons:

• From after being abandoned by the Qing dynasty to the century of British colonial rule, and from the trauma of the Cultural Revolution to the memory of the Tiananmen Square massacre, people in Hong Kong never truly identified with China. A survey in June 2014 reveals that only 31 percent of people in Hong Kong considered themselves Chinese, while 40 percent identified as Hong Kongers.

• In recent years, violent incidents in Hong Kong, such as the attack on the chief editor of Ming Pao newspaper, and media self-censorship have made people in Hong Kong feel oppressed, believing such incidents were posing a threat to their freedom.

• The status of its international financial center and free port once brought immense pride to Hong Kong as part of China but not entirely Chinese. However, this unique status had already vanished and the sense of pride from the past had disappeared.

• Livelihood issues are also a significant factor: the housing problem caused by the dominance of the real estate sector, intergenerational inequalities, soaring prices, and declining living standards. The benefits of economic growth have mainly been concentrated among a small number of vested interests, while small and medium-sized enterprises struggle to thrive. Hong Kong's wealth gap has reached 21.15 (the ratio of the highest 20 percent of household disposable income to the lowest 20 percent), which is higher than that in Taiwan by over six times and that in South Korea by over five times. With a population of over 7 million, more than 1.3 million people, half of whom have jobs and are known as the "working poor," live below the poverty line. The United Nations has singled out Hong Kong as the place with the most severe wealth gap in Asia and the highest rate of people living below the poverty line.

• The failure to achieve genuine universal suffrage was the final straw that bankrupted the "one country, two systems" principle, leading to Hong Kong people's disappointment turning into despair. The method for selecting the Chief Executive was originally based on Annex I of the Basic Law. According to Article 7 of Annex I, if changes to the method of selecting the Chief Executive were needed after 2007, approval would be required from two-thirds of the Legislative Council, agreement by the Chief Executive, and endorsement by the Standing Committee of the National People's Congress (NPC) in Beijing. This was known as a "three-step process." However, in 2004, the NPC Standing Committee broke its promise and issued a supplementary interpretation, adding two more steps: the Chief

Executive was to report to the NPC Standing Committee on whether such changes were needed and the Standing Committee had the authority to make a determination according to the Basic Law and the principle of gradual progress. This became the "five-step process," thereby bankrupting the "one country, two systems" policy. On August 30, 2014, the NPC Standing Committee added the requirement of "patriots governing Hong Kong" and approval of over half of the Nomination Committee, thus further limiting democratic choice. This is the background to the despair among people of Hong Kong who see this as a process of screening rather than genuine universal suffrage.

• The emergence and growth of the number of members of the younger generations: They no longer prioritize stability and order, nor do they focus solely on economic concerns, and they cannot tolerate the absence of democracy. The members of the older generations could tolerate this because they had witnessed the transition from nothing to what Hong Kong had become. However, for the members of the younger generations, it has been a transition from having to losing. This anger cannot be understood by the older generations.

• Dissatisfaction with Leung Chun-ying: In the past, there were officials left over from the British era, such as like Anson Chan and Donald Tsang, for whom the Hong Kong people still had a certain amount of trust. However, Leung Chun-ying was perceived to be a member of the Chinese Communist Party (CCP), and his reputation was far below that of the former chief executive, Donald Tsang. After the CCP forced Tsang to step down, Hong Kong people had a sense of distrust toward his successor Leung Chun-ying. Simultaneously, the pro-democracy camp split, which was also disappointing. It could not achieve a significant presence in the Legislative Council to provide effective checks and balances. The people had no source of support, so they had to stand up for themselves.

• More recently, tensions between Hong Kong people and mainland Chinese have deepened due to incidents such as the uncivilized behavior by mainland tourists and the issue of non-resident pregnant women giving birth in Hong Kong as well as disputes over the Chinese buying up of baby formula and the introduction of "national education" in schools.

• The backlash against the CCP's hardline stance, which also reflected changes within China, such as the provocative statement in the "One Country, Two Systems White Paper" that "you have as many rights as the CCP grants you," and the more stringent 2014 NPC Standing Committee decision on election of the chief executive. This a hardline approach has led to more despair among Hong Kong people, pushing them on the path of resistance.

In summary, "a three-foot thick layer of ice does not form in a single day." Therefore, resolving these issues in the short term will also be impossible.

Question 47: Why did the "One Country, Two Systems" completely fail?

In Hong Kong, 15-year-old high school student Joshua Wong founded the "Scholarism" organization to oppose the Hong Kong government's attempt to enforce a pro-CCP, pro-China model, and to cover up major historical events like the Tiananmen Square massacre through its program of so-called "national education." In my view, the outbreak of anti–"national education" and anti-Communist sentiment in Hong Kong represented not merely single isolated events but rather the cumulative eruption of long-suppressed grievances and anxieties. It was also a consequence of the increasingly tense relationship between Hong Kong and mainland China in recent years.

From a historical perspective, Hong Kong's anti-Communist sentiments have deep roots and have been steadily strengthening. This can be explained by four issues:

First, having been a British colony for a century, Hong Kong lacks a long-standing emotional connection with the mainland in terms of historical legacy. The social systems and values planted by the British are deeply rooted in Hong Kong and cannot be easily replaced within ten or twenty years.

Second, many people in the 50–60 age group arrived in Hong Kong during the period before and after the Cultural Revolution. Most had fled to Hong Kong due to political persecution and harsh living conditions on the mainland. For them, coming to

Hong Kong was an act of voting with their feet, representing their dissatisfaction with the Chinese Communist Party (CCP). Now, in the face of prospects of CCP rule again, their inner resistance is understandable. In this movement, some banners were displayed with the message, "We escaped brainwashing back then, we can't repeat history today," expressing such sentiments.

Third, the trauma of the Tiananmen Square massacre is an essential part of the collective psychology of Hong Kong people. Tiananmen Square is like a sacred object and it is the most sensitive nerve center for Hong Kong people, something that must not be touched lightly. In 1989, Hong Kong people already knew that reunification would be inevitable, and they were anxious about their future. At that critical moment, the Tiananmen Square massacre led to great fear among Hong Kong people. This historical wound runs deep, making Hong Kong people attach significant importance to the issue. The fact that the proposed "national education" in Hong Kong omitted any mention of the Tiananmen Square massacre was bound to trigger a strong backlash.

Furthermore, in recent years, the human rights situation in China has deteriorated to an unprecedented level. Liu Xiaobo received an eleven-year prison sentence merely for drafting critical articles about the government on the internet. The suspicious death of Li Wangyang, ruled a "suicide" by the authorities, left Hong Kong people feeling that after all these years there has been no real change in the government and all their earlier hopes and expectations had been in vain, leading to a sense of anger and indignation. This special concern for the human rights situation in China is, in fact, influenced by the lingering memories and emotions related to the Tiananmen Square incident.

Fourth, in recent years, as exchanges between mainland China and Hong Kong have become more frequent, conflicts arising from the different cultural backgrounds, social systems, and values have become increasingly prominent. Hong Kong people find it difficult to accept the behavior and actions by mainlanders in Hong Kong. Issues like "birth tourism," concerning mainland pregnant Chinese women who come to Hong Kong to give birth, have fueled dissatisfaction among Hong Kong residents based on solid conflicts of interest. The statement made by Professor Kong Qingdong from the Chinese Department of Peking University, calling Hong Kong people "dogs," further ignited the dissatisfaction. The anti–"national education" movement can thus also be seen as a culmination of the conflict between Hong Kong and mainland Chinese societies in recent years.

In conclusion, the movement initiated by three high school students captured the attention and consensus of Hong Kong society and mobilized support from the entire civil society and various parties, with even experienced activists from the 1970s joining the hunger strike. The atmosphere in Hong Kong was boiling due to the long-term accumulation of grievances. Therefore, the Hong Kong government's temporary concessions regarding the "national education" issue did not solve the problem.

From the beginning, "One Country, Two Systems" was merely a temporary measure with more of an element of deception than of sincerity, mainly aimed at placating the people in Hong Kong. The patience of the CCP is gradually wearing thin. Promotion of the so-called "national education" was actually a requirement by Hu Jintao during the 15th-anniversary celebration of the Hong Kong handover. It is evident that the CCP no longer wants to play the role of "guardian" under "One Country, Two Systems"; it is determined to tear down the facade of "One Country, Two Systems." This is thus the first clear sign of the complete failure of "One Country, Two Systems."

Another proof of its failure lies in the fact that "One Country, Two Systems" was designed to exchange time for space. During the period of "One Country, Two Systems," the CCP gradually attempted to infiltrate Hong Kong ideologically and establish control over public opinion through a gradual approach, without actually returning Hong Kong to the people's hearts. This was to avoid Hong Kong continuing to serve as an anti-Communist base. However, in recent years, the rise of the "90s generation" in Hong Kong has completely shattered Beijing's expectations. These young people, who were not even born during the Tiananmen Square massacre, hold strong animosity toward the CCP and its ideology. Their Tiananmen Square massacre sentiments far exceed that of the members of the previous generations, which is probably something that Beijing did not anticipate. The gradual reclamation of the hearts of Hong Kong people through "One Country, Two Systems" has entirely failed.

In conclusion, the real problem lies in the failure of "One Country, Two Systems" and the failure of the CCP's ruling model. In simple terms, the development model represented by the CCP, collectively known as the "China model," prioritizes economic growth above all else, sacrificing democratic freedoms in society to expand economic power. In contrast, the social development model advocated by civil society in Hong Kong and Taiwan prioritizes human dignity and freedom, social justice, and tolerance as the purpose of economic development. The two models have fundamentally different definitions of "happiness."

Despite Hong Kong's return to the mainland, today it is displaying its most significant dissatisfaction with China since 2003. Furthermore, the results of an identity survey of Hong Kong people toward China has reached a new low. The survey conducted by the University of Hong Kong in May 2012 shows that the level of discontent with the Chinese government among Hong Kong people had increased from 25 percent in November of the previous year to 37 percent, while favorable impressions of the mainland had decreased from 29 percent to 20 percent. Another survey, conducted by Hong Kong Baptist University's "Hong Kong Transition Project," which interviewed over 900 Hong Kong citizens, revealed that 40 percent identified themselves as Chinese, while 27 percent identified as "Hong Kong Chinese" and 17 percent identified as "Hong Kong people." However, among the young population between the ages of 18 and 29, only 4 percent identified as Chinese, and the figure was 0 percent for students above 18 years old. The survey also indicated that 62 percent of civil servants were dissatisfied or very dissatisfied with the government's performance, and 76 percent believed that the government policies were unfair or very unfair. These survey data are clear evidence of the complete failure of the "One Country, Two Systems" policy.

Moreover, during the 2012 presidential election in Taiwan, China's blatant intervention through Taiwanese businesses and pro-China media showed signs of the "Hong Kong-ization" of Taiwan. The civil societies in Taiwan and Hong Kong, which used to have only distant relations, have begun to pay attention to each other. The development of civil society in mainland China will likely determine the future destiny of both Hong Kong and Taiwan. How the civil societies in these three regions combine and interact in the future is something worth serious consideration and exploration.

Question 48: Why is the Xinjiang issue a powder keg?

The U.S. Congress has convened a series of hearings on the theme "China's Challenges." The most notable revelation was the severity of the ethnic persecution carried out by the Chinese government in Xinjiang. If the accusations made by the United States may be biased, the United Nations, which has deep ties to China, has provided strong evidence of some of the accusations during a meeting of the Committee on the Elimination of Racial Discrimination (CERD) in Geneva on August 10, 2019.

CERD Committee member Gay McDougall stated during the meeting, "We have received many credible reports indicating that China has turned the Xinjiang Uighur Autonomous Region into a secretive large-scale labor camp under the guise of combating religious extremism and maintaining stability. We are deeply concerned about this." McDougall estimated that about two million Uighurs and Muslims in Xinjiang were being detained in "political re-education camps." The disclosure of this data shocked the world, and after a prolonged period of silence, the Xinjiang issue has become a focal point of concern.

The severity of the Xinjiang issue today far surpasses what was expected, resulting in the Chinese authorities resorting to military control in Xinjiang, which undoubtedly exacerbates the conflict. It is not an exaggeration to say that the Xinjiang issue in China is a powder keg, with the potential to erupt into large-scale violent conflict at any moment.

To understand in-depth the context of the Xinjiang issue, David Eimer's book The Emperor Far Away: Travels at the Edge of China provides many clues. In the 1930s, the Indigenous people of Xinjiang began using the term "Uighur." Before that, their self-identity was limited to their regional affiliations, such as Urumqi people, Kashgar people, or Hotan people. In 1947, the total number of Han people in Xinjiang was only 220,000, but now there are over eight million Han people, accounting for more than 40 percent of the total population. The migration process was neither natural nor smooth. Statistics show that in the 1950s alone, up to 60,000 Uighurs died resisting rule by Beijing and during the so-called "eradication of superstition" campaign. It is evident that state violence has played a key role in the process of the Han-ification in Xinjiang, leaving a deep wound in the hearts of Uighur people.

In my view, the authorities' gradual Han-ification policy, using a "boiled frog" approach, has not only intensified conflicts between Uighurs and Han Chinese but has also deepened the Uighurs' concerns and anxieties about ethnic survival. These concerns and anxieties will undoubtedly be expressed through a renewed understanding and reinforcement of their ethnic identity. In particular, Xinjiang is bordered by three neighboring Central Asian independent countries and interactions between Uighurs in Xinjiang and those in these three countries are much more frequent than the Uighurs' interactions with Han Chinese. This serves as a reminder of the possibility of independence for Uighur people. The historical entanglements, the influence of current policies, and the surrounding environment all contribute to the fundamental conflict in the Xinjiang issue.

Facing such a complex issue in Xinjiang, the Chinese authorities have surprisingly resorted to large-scale concentration camps and comprehensive "ideological transformation" as a means of control. On the surface, it seems they are using a tough approach to suppress Uighur resistance, but in reality, this is indicative of the dilemma facing the Chinese Communist Party (CCP). The party cannot find a better way to prevent the deterioration of the Xinjiang crisis, so it resorts to brute force. I believe that the Chinese authorities themselves are well aware that using military control to handle ethnic conflicts is not the best choice and in fact may be the worst choice. However, in this seemingly hopeless situation, resorting to this worst option might ignite the most significant crisis in the Xinjiang issue.

During China's modernization process, ethnic issues and separatism have been inevitable. Scholars have pointed out that under the pressures of modernization, globalization, and urbanization, ethnic minorities may face more cultural challenges than the Han majority, leading them to more urgently cling to their ethnicity, religion, and regional affiliations, thereby giving this identity higher social importance. In other words, the emergence of ethnic issues is largely due to issues of identity or deeper cultural problems. These problems cannot be solved simply by providing economic support or imposing political control. In my view, the failure to recognize this issue, or the unwillingness to address the Xinjiang issue from this perspective, is the main reason why the Xinjiang issue has evolved into a thorny problem for the CCP.

David Eimer's book The Emperor Far Away: Travels at the Edge of China reveals through firsthand observations the specific manifestations of the CCP's simplistic governance of Xinjiang, such as prohibiting those under 18 years old from participating in mosque prayers, mandating that Han men working in government institutions must not have beards, or requiring that all ethnic groups in Xinjiang attend school together with Han people. Additionally, in September 2014, the most influential Uighur scholar in China, Ilham Tohti, was sentenced to life imprisonment on charges of separatism. Tohti, only 44 years old at the time, was a scholar nurtured by the CCP and had long taught at Minzu University of China in Beijing. He was a moderate nationalist who advocated unity, opposed separatism, condemned violence, and had asserted that "Xinjiang independence has no future." He promoted the rule of law and ethnic autonomy. But instead of being a bridge for communication between the central government and the separatist forces in Xinjiang, or even between Uighurs and Han Chinese, his mild opposition led to his heavy sentence, which only exacerbated the contradictions in Xinjiang. Wang Lequan's rule as party secretary in Xinjiang between 1994 and 2010, using high-pressure suppression tactics, did not solve the Xinjiang issue and instead made it worse, demonstrating that the effectiveness of political repression could backfire.

So, how does the CCP's focus on economics fare as a solution?

After Wang Lequan, Zhang Chunxian was appointed by the

central government to govern Xinjiang as party secretary. His basic approach was to use economic means to rule the area. Specifically, he sought to align the developed regions in the east with various prefectures in Xinjiang to promote economic development through investments from the East. However, David Eimer's investigation tells us that economic development, if accompanied by distributional issues, sometimes not only will fail to ease local social conflicts but also will become an additional source of contradictions. For example, in Xinjiang's prosperous oil and gas industry, which accounts for over half of its gross production value, Uighurs make up only 1 percent of the labor force. Southern Xinjiang is the heartland of Uighurs, where agriculture is the primary industry. Most of Southern Xinjiang is the Taklamakan Desert, which is completely unsuitable for farming, so an increasing number of Uighurs are choosing to follow the model of Han farmers in other parts of China: moving to cities to seek higher-paying jobs. But Uighurs receive insufficient education and cannot speak Mandarin fluently, making it challenging for them to find jobs. Many of the rioters in the 2009 riots came from the pool of newly arrived migrants from the rural areas. These problems can well explain why the central government's substantial investments in Xinjiang, with the hope of easing ethnic conflicts through economic development, have not been highly effective.

The Xinjiang issue at its core boils down to the Beijing authorities' inability to address and confront the most profound aspect of the problem, that is, how to positively manage issues of identity stemming from cultural and historical origins.

Question 49: Is the Tibet issue really unsolvable?

The 2014 Kunming incident once again brought China's increasingly serious regional ethnic conflicts to the world's attention, making the so-called borderland issues, including Tibet, a nationwide concern. Faced with the prospect of escalating violence, apart from condemning the excessive killing of innocent civilians by extremist forces, the long-standing ethnic policies implemented by the Chinese Communist Party (CCP) also need to be subject to scrutiny. Otherwise, a simple fact cannot be explained: why have the crackdowns on separatist forces in Xinjiang and Tibet in recent years only resulted in an increase in violent attacks?

Regarding the CCP's long-standing policies toward ethnic minorities, the core issue is whether "high autonomy" has been genuinely implemented in Xinjiang and Tibet. I believe that, first, the majority in Xinjiang and Tibet do not advocate complete independence at this stage. Second, however, widespread discontent exists with the central government's ethnic policies. So, from where does this dissatisfaction stem? The main problem is the authorities' insincerity in granting genuine autonomy to for those in the ethnic regions, particularly for the Uighur and Tibetan people.

This criticism of the CCP's ethnic policies is not only limited to opposition figures; even within the top echelons of the party, there have been similar views. One prominent figure was Hu Yaobang, who served as general secretary of the CCP in the 1980s.

According to The Biography of Hu Jintao and Deng Liqun's memoirs, in 1980, during a visit to the outskirts of Lhasa to inspect the living conditions of some residents living in communes, Hu Yaobang was shocked by the extremely dire living conditions of the Tibetan people. He questioned the Tibetan officials in person, asking, "Have all the special funds allocated by the central government to aid Tibet been thrown into the Yarlung Tsangpo River?" He sorrowfully remarked that the disastrous consequences of the extreme leftist policies implemented by the predominantly Han Chinese authorities in Tibet were akin to "colonial practices."

On May 29, 1980, Hu Yaobang delivered a speech at a conference of officials in the Tibet Autonomous Region. He summarized his speech in six words: "Exemption from taxes, relaxing control, and withdrawal of personnel." The phrase "withdrawal of personnel" referred to a substantial withdrawal of Han Chinese officials from Tibet, thereby allowing the proportion of Tibetan officials to become an absolute majority. He said, "Within two to three years, preferably within two years, the country's cadre personnel, including teachers, should be made up of two-thirds Tibetan; those who are not cadre personnel must all be Tibetans." He also emphasized the need to arrange for Han Chinese cadres in Tibet to return home, ensuring that the central government, Han Chinese cadres, Tibetan cadres, and the people all would be satisfied with this approach. He asked, "With satisfaction by all three sides, why shouldn't we proceed with this?

However, Hu Yaobang's proposal faced strong opposition from the hardliners within the party, especially from those Han Chinese officials who had worked in Tibet for a long time. They strongly objected, stating that once Han Chinese officials were withdrawn, separatist forces would inevitably grow. As a result, Hu Yaobang's policy was not adopted by top CCP leader Deng Xiaoping. It is clear that a huge interest group had already formed around China's Tibet policy, and they would use stability as an excuse to safeguard their own interests. Stability, for the CCP, is a trump card; once played, other proposals must take a backseat. Of course, as we can see now, rejecting Hu Yaobang's proposal in the name of stability did not lead to a more stable situation in Tibet.

I bring up this historical account to demonstrate that even within the CCP, there were instances when some in the CCP recognized the problem of failing to implement genuine ethnic autonomy, and they attempted to improve the situation. However, such progressive policies were unable to pass the mainstream "leftists" in the CCP. Perhaps, in light of the increasingly serious issues in Xinjiang and Tibet today, it is necessary to revisit Hu Yaobang's ideas regarding ethnic policy.

Conclusions

Question 50: What will cause the collapse of China's authoritarian regime?

Regarding a collapse of China, many scholars who consider themselves objective and rational do not think a collapse will occur. They believe that such claims of a potential collapse are made by people who are anti-Communist and these individuals who criticize China's development because of their own dissatisfaction with the Communist Party, making their ideas untrustworthy. They forget that historically, even massive authoritarian empires like the former Soviet Union, have suddenly collapsed even when almost no one believed it could happen . So why couldn't the same thing take place in China as well? With a historical perspective, one should know that every authoritarian system ultimately ends in collapse. Why should China be an exception?

Those who claim that Communist Party rule will not collapse are making a very naive mistake: they consider events that have not yet happened as certain to never happen. It is like telling passengers in a car on a clear and smooth road that a car accident is about to happen – of course, they will think you are ridiculous. However, we all know that the absence of a car accident does not mean there will never be an accident in the future. Many who could not believe that the Soviet Union would collapse now ignore the fact that it has indeed collapsed and they refuse to believe that CCP rule might end as well.

In my view, rule by authoritarian regimes is inevitably destined to collapse. If the Chinese Communist Party (CCP) does not change its authoritarian model of governance, it too will inevitably collapse., even if we cannot provide specific details about how or when the collapse will occur. Why do authoritarian regimes collapse? This is a question I seek to explore below.

The book In Search of China by He Wei, based on the author's experience of traveling across much of China, reveals the shocking reality about life at the bottom rungs of Chinese society. The book is often referred to as the Chinese version of On the Road by Jack Kerouac. Together with the author's other two works, Oracle Bones and The Vanishing City of Jiang, the three books form a trilogy that represents one of the best serious observations of Chinese society in recent years by a foreign writer. The book contains the following detailed anecdote that has rich symbolism:

The author was once stopped by several highway patrol officers while driving, and the following scene unfolded: "You must be a spy!" the officer said. The others laughed and joined in. "He's a spy! He drives around, he can speak Chinese – he must be a spy! Spy! Spy!" The police officers shook with laughter as they handed back my driver's licenses. It took me a while to speak. "Can I continue on the road?" "Of course, you can!" As I drove away, I saw the police playing by the side of the road. They were shoving each other and laughing, "Spy! Spy!"

This amusing anecdote reveals some profound truths: Let us discuss the absurdity of the logic that the authorities had instilled in these police officers.

"Driving around, speaking Chinese, so he must be a spy." The key is that when the police officers said the word "spy," the author was so nervous that he could not utter even a word. However, the police officers did not carry out any action related to this characterization of him, such as detention, interrogation, or even checking more documents; they simply waved him on and let him go. On the one hand, they called him a spy, but on the other, they laughed and let him go. This is even more absurd than the previous logic, and the ultimate reason authoritarian regimes collapse lies in this "absurdity within an absurdity." Why do I say this?

First, the governing logic of authoritarian regimes is so absurd that even the regime's enforcers themselves regard it as a joke when faced with the concrete reality. Think about China today. Its so-called "socialism," the claim that "the Communist Party serves the people," and the notion of "common prosperity" – how many Communist Party officials genuinely believe all this lofty rhetoric? The officials just repeat without conviction, and they themselves do not believe it. If Xi Jinping honestly believed that Western social and education systems were "hypocritical," he would not have sent his daughter to study at

Harvard University. This shows that even Xi does not believe in the education system he promotes. History tells us that when a system's basic theories are no longer believed, not even by their proponents, it becomes difficult to maintain them. Therefore, the first reason for the collapse of authoritarianism is that the governing logic has become too absurd to be taken seriously.

Milan Kundera authored a famous novel called The Joke, which portrays this idea. Interested readers can explore the profound satire in the book; the authoritarian regime he describes has already collapsed.

Second, on the surface, China's stability maintenance system is vast and rigorous, and social control is pervasive. There are so many elements involved, even to the point where one must provide real-name information to buy a kitchen knife during sensitive periods. In theory, such a system should not collapse. However, why have all authoritarian regimes in history eventually collapsed? The reason is simple: no matter how strict the system, it still relies on implementation by individuals. When individuals no longer rigorously believe in the system, the system collapses. Consider that even with the massive stability maintenance apparatus in China, who can guarantee that no individual will make a mistake? Once one person loses control, it might trigger public anger, and this is why the Chinese government is always on edge. This is also an inherent reason why all authoritarian regimes in history eventually collapsed.

The hypocritical ideology promoted by the CCP has created a

distorted phenomenon among officialdom. There is a humorous saying that accurately describes this situation: "On the job, they are members of the CCP, but off the job, they are democrats." This means that CCP officials speak officially during working hours but express grievances, speak negatively, and criticize the system when off-duty, often to the point of becoming opponents of the regime.

To clearly understand the mindset of CCP officials, one must recognize the impact of the Cultural Revolution and the Tiananmen Square protests on Chinese people's thinking. These events led to a loss of faith in the Communist Party's ideological propaganda. The social reality exists in a stark contrast to this extreme hypocrisy. But CCP officials cannot exist independently of the society. They see and understand the problems with the system in areas such as rule of law, income inequality, and rampant corruption, perhaps even more clearly than the average person. However, because of their vested interests, they continue to rely on and support the system.

For instance, looking at the situation when lawyer Gao Zhisheng was trapped in Shaanxi and later forcibly returned to Beijing, local officials used thuggish means to drive him out of Shaanxi. However, in private, they expressed their understanding of Gao Zhisheng's actions, attributing their actions to being compelled by higher-ups and requesting understanding from Gao's family. A bureau chief even revealed to Gao Zhisheng's family that the local government had invited a professor from China University of Political Science and Law to give a lecture, but the lecture turned into a criticism session of CCP misrule, making the situation uncomfortable for the party secretary and mayor who were present. The police officers who monitored Gao Zhisheng openly told him, "You don't need to talk reason with us; we are just hooligans." This is perhaps an unprecedented case in which officials publicly proclaim themselves to be hooligans, demonstrating that even those tasked with upholding the CCP regime have started to face those being persecuted with a degree of empathy.

Moreover, many officials have made it clear that if a protest movement were to take place, they would join in. Although these officials' attitudes may not represent the attitudes of all CCP{officials, it is evident that a growing number of officials no longer dare to confront the persecuted; they continue their evasion and remain unwilling to stake their own futures on such a brutal regime.

This phenomenon of evasion is driven by their inner conflict. They see the system as inhumane and flawed. They fear for the future, not only for themselves but also for their descendants who will have to live in China. They understand that the future of China is deeply connected to their own futures. In this regard, their thinking is fundamentally different from that of the few high-ranking CCP officials who have already secured their interests abroad and have the option to emigrate. Therefore, as the "democratic" side of these officials grows stronger, we can expect that more and more officials will begin speaking the truth when they are not on duty.

When these CCP leaders begin opposing their own "Communist" side in their actions, the arrival of a truly harmonious society will not be far off. Chinese society seems to be quietly preparing for the moment when the time is ripe. This is another reason why I believe CCP rule in China will inevitably collapse.

渠成文化　王丹自選輯 9

The fifty questions on China

作　　者 Wang Dan ｜王丹
出版單位 匠心文化創意行銷有限公司

發 行 人 陳錦德
出版總監 柯延婷
專案企劃 謝政均
美術設計 顏柯夫
內頁設計 顏柯夫
編輯校對 匠心文創
E-mail cxwc0801@gmail.com
網址 https://www.facebook.com/CXWC0801
出版日期 2023 年 12 月初版一刷
總代理旭昇圖書有限公司
地址新北市中和區中山路二段 352 號 2 樓電話 02-2245-1480(代表號)
印製安隆印刷
定價新臺幣 450 元
ISBN　978-626-97301-7-9